JOURNEY FROM BROOKLYN

Dr. DAVID GARRAHAN

MAPLE LEAF
PUBLISHING INC.

Journey From Brooklyn
Copyright © 2022 by David Garrahan (Revised Edition)

All rights reserved. No part of this book may be reproduced or transmitted, downloaded, distributed, reverse engineered, or stored in or introduced into any information storage and retrieval system, in any form or by any means, including photocopying and recording, whether electronic or mechanical, now known or hereinafter invented without permission in writing from the publisher.

DISCLAIMER: The contents of this work, including, but not limited to, the accuracy of events, people, and places depicted; opinions expressed; permission to use previously published materials included; and any advice given or actions advocated are solely the responsibility of the author, who assumes all liability for said work and indemnifies the publisher against any claims stemming from publication of the work.

Revised Edition Publishing by Maple Leaf Publishing Inc.

Publication Date: April 21, 2022

To order additional copies of this book, please contact:

MAPLE LEAF PUBLISHING INC.
www.mapleleafpublishinginc.com
3rd Floor 4915 54 St Red Deer, Alberta T4N 2G7 Canada

General Inquiries & Customer Service
Phone: 1-(403)-356-0255
Toll Free: 1-(888)-498-9380
Email: info@mapleleafpublishinginc.com

ISBN Paperback: 978-1774191699
ISBN eBook: 978-1774191583

Also by David Garrahan

Collegiate Compensatory Programs for Disadvantaged Youth

Transition America

From Brooklyn to Kingsport

Brooklyn Bred

Destiny Control

An abridged but unexpurgated edition

TABLE OF CONTENTS

FORWARD v

CHAPTER 1 – MY LIFE IN 1940'S BROOKLYN 1

CHAPTER 2 – FROM BROOKLYN TO THE FARM 23

CHAPTER 3 – FROM FARM TO YACHT CLUB 37

CHAPTER 4 – I'M IN COLLEGE 45

CHAPTER 5 – COLLEGE GRADUATE…. MARRIED 52

CHAPTER 6 – DOCTORAL STUDY
     AT COLUMBIA UNIVERSITY 64

CHAPTER 7 – FROM COLUMBIA UNIVERSITY
     TO FROSTBURG STATE UNIVERSITY 84

CHAPTER 8 – GARRAHAN RETIRES 90

CHAPTER 9 – END OF MY JOURNEY 108

AFTERWORD 121

APPENDIX 123

FORWARD

Journey From Brooklyn is an autobiography, the history of my life from age 2 to 84. It has not been professionally edited. Institutions and individuals are identified. I name the sexual predator who I dismissed. He is still active, and may sue me...but I have the audio tapes.

I, alone, accept complete liability, including cold-case exposure. If the man I stabbed in 2013 died, I can be prosecuted(see Afterword).

Thanks to Ryan Brackenrig at ServiceByte for his tech support,including placing the color photographs with captions.

Chapter 1

MY LIFE IN 1940'S BROOKLYN

We all make zillions of decisions over our lifespan, most are inconsequential. In these pages attention is focused on consequential decisions that I made which shaped my life's journey. You will learn that my decision to scream to my sister, "run to the police station" as I attempted to disarm my mother was consequential. Had I made a different decision (or no decision), it is likely that this book would not have been written. Decisions have consequences... every decision.

Throughout my life, as I approached a 'fork in the road', I thought about my decision-and tried to anticipate the likely implications. This strategic decision making behavior reflects a personality of internal control on Rotter's Locus of Control continuum.

My earliest memory of my father was when my brother, Artie, and were on a bus somewhere between Brooklyn and Pennsylvania. It was 1940. The bus stopped, and people stood up to leave. Looking at me, my father said, "Let's go, shake a leg". Artie walked in front of me; Dad was behind me. We followed the people getting off the bus. When I got to the front, a man in a uniform lifted me up, and set me on the ground. Dad looked at me and yelled, "What are you doing?" Artie answered, "Dad, he's doing what you told him to do. He's shaking his legs". We probably went inside to a bathroom. I must have wondered where Mom was. Later I would learn that she was in a mental hospital. I woke up in a strange house. It was 1202 Mine Street, located in Old Forge, PA.

There were a lot of people living in the house. Artie and I could not understand what they were saying in a foreign language. All of a sudden, Dad was gone! In the 1940 photo, Artie and I appear to be well dressed and well fed, though I cannot recall any details of our stay at the house. Children can be seen watching us from a distance. (see photo)

Back to Brooklyn

At about age three, I ended up back at our home at 293 Oakland Street, in the Greenpoint section of Brooklyn. Mom and Dad were there. The building was five stories tall, with two families living on each level. All the apartments (railroad-flats), and all the buildings (tenements) were the same. In October 1941, Loretta was born.

Dad worked on the docks. World War II was raging. Dad would often have to work 'around the clock', as he told Mom. Sometimes he would be gone for two or three days.

It was a scary time. There were frequent air raid drills called 'black outs'. I had to wear a dog tag on a chain around my neck. Once, an air raid warden banged on our door, entered, and yelled at my father to never have a light on when the air raid sirens were sounding. Mom explained to Artie and me that with no lights on, a Japanese pilot would not be able to see any target. Dad always sat at the kitchen table, reading the newspaper or listening to his radio, smoking his Camel cigarettes, and drinking beer.

Mom and Dad Fight

Mom would tell Dad to come home right after work. Often, he didn't, and when he would come home, Mom would often tell him that she smelled whiskey on his breath. Sometimes, there would be a fight. He would give her some money from his wallet, and she would yell that it wasn't enough to pay the rent and to buy food. Dad would throw a few more bills at Mom, grab his jacket, and leave. Once she threw a heavy iron at him as he slammed the door shut, and it broke the glass top of the door. The wire mesh inside the glass held it together. Mom asked the landlord, Mr. Yourga, to fix it, but he never did. Sometimes the police would come down the hallway yelling, "Police! Police! Trouble"! They knew to come to our door, apartment 1-A. I was glad when they came to end the fighting, but they never could. They would always say, "No more fighting. If the problem continues, go to family court," and hand Mom a card. She never went to court.

Once during a fight, Dad broke off the bottom of his beer bottle and went at Mom. I ran behind him and kicked the bottle as hard as I could. Blood came out of the tear in my sneaker, and the fighting stopped. I'm reminded of that fight when I see the scar it left on my foot.

Dad did other things that bothered me. Once I went down the wooden steps into the cellar. When I got to the bottom, I could see Dad kneeling on the floor doing something with our kittens. Artie and I had waited a long time for our mother cat to have her kittens. As I walked closer, I could see that Dad had tied all the kittens around a brick, and was lowering them into a pail of water. I could hardly believe my eyes. He yelled at me, "Get the hell out of here!"

At times, he did good things. One day, I went down to the cellar, and saw Dad up on a ladder doing something with our electric meter. He showed me how to open the glass cover on the meter, and to press a penny in a certain spot inside the box. When we went upstairs, we had electricity in our apartment!

Mr. and Mrs. Frayer lived next door to us in apartment 1-B. Sometimes, Mrs. Frayer would come over, and talk to Mom about the noise and the fighting. She would also ask Mom to pray for her son, Jimmy, who was in the army. One day I was sitting on the front stoop when two soldiers came up the steps. They walked down the hallway. Then I heard screaming. The Frayers' only child, Jimmy, had been killed in the war. The death of their son changed the Frayers' lives. Mr. Frayer would get drunk, and fall down in the hallway. I had never seen him like that before. After he died, Mrs. Frayer moved out of their apartment, and into an apartment on nearby India Street.

When Dad went to work, Artie and I would walk up to the India Street subway station at the end of the day. We would wait, as the subway trains came in, to see if we spotted him in the crowd. For some strange reason, when Dad didn't come home from work, Mom would beat us. Once she hit Artie so hard, blood came out of his ear. Loretta was always spared from these beatings. [Flash Forward to 1976: Years later, I asked Mom why she beat me and Artie so much when we were children. She explained that she thought that if we screamed loud enough, "your father would hear you. and come home"!]

Ready for School

Dad walked me to my first day of school at St. Anthony of Padua School. I never did find out why we had been sent to a Catholic school. Never in my life had I seen my mother or father in a church—not even once! When we got close to the school, Dad said, "Don't take any guff. If you have to fight, go for the nose. When he sees his blood, he'll stop fighting." He told Brother Irenaeus that I was "as smart as a whip".

The boys at the school were taught by Franciscan Brothers. They were very strict. The girls, were taught by the Sisters of St. Joseph, and were kept in an entirely separate part of the large building. We were instructed to never set foot in that section. I did, however, and got caught by the principal. I pretended that I had gotten lost in the hallways. We went to confession every Saturday, and received the Holy Eucharist on Sunday. This was obligatory for all students. The Mass was always said in Latin. I was involved in religion seven days a week… for eight years!

The Fighting Irish

I got into my first fight in first grade. I don't remember what Patrick Burkrey and I fought about, or who started it. Maybe I thought he was "giving me guff". I do remember how it ended, with Fat Pat on top of me, banging me into the cobblestone street. In second grade, I started a fight with Richard Eaton. It didn't last long. He threw me all over the place. Brother Brian marched us into the building where he gave us a good beating with a wooden paddle. In fourth grade, a kid grabbed the white sailor hat off my head, and threw it to another kid. Soon there were about five kids involved. Every time I ran to grab my hat, it would be thrown to another kid. My hat was getting dirty, so I waited until the smallest kid, Edmund Orlowski, caught my hat. Then I pounced on him, punching him until he let go of my hat, and I fell on top of him on the curb.

Brother Alexis blew a single whistle, which meant that we were to march into the school. I left Edmund lying on the curb. Brother Alexis had not noticed him. Later, the Principal, Brother Irenaeus, came into my classroom, walked me into his office, closed the door, and asked, "were you fighting with Edmund?" I said that he had my hat. The Brother said, "That's not what I asked", as he struck me in the face repeatedly. When my nose started bleeding, he stopped, and told me to return to his office at the end of the school day.

Edmund had been taken to the hospital. He had a broken ankle. I was ordered to visit him at his home every day with a gift until he returned to school. It was a long time before he could walk to school, but I brought him a different comic book every day. All the kids traded comics with each other, so I kept getting new comics for Edmund. Finally, he was able to walk, but he always walked with a limp after that.

Franciscan Brothers wore black, hooded habits (robes) which went from the top of their heads down to their black shoes. They had white ropes fastened around their waists. They carried a string of large black rosary beads in a pocket, which they would touch and say prayers with repeatedly, as they walked up and down the sidewalk in front of the school. I remember wondering, if it was normal for Brothers to never get married and have children.

The Brothers were advocates of corporal punishment. At times, it was both abusive and unwarranted. For example, in sixth grade, we were dutifully lined up in the street waiting for Brother Cipriani to blow the whistle which was our signal to begin walking into the building. However, he stepped off the sidewalk, walked straight to me and without saying a word, he struck me in the face with such force that it knocked me backwards into the student behind me. I asked the kid, "Why did he hit me?" He whispered, "You had your hands in your pockets?"

Once in religion class, I asked, "How long is eternity?" Brother Cipriani began his answer by asking me what the circumference of planet earth was. "Thousands of miles", I replied. He told me to picture in my mind, a steel ball the size of the earth. Then he told me to picture a white dove flying down, sweeping its wing on the surface of the steel earth, and flying back into the sky. One year later the dove returned, and again swept its wing on the earth's surface. Each year, the bird's wing would rub against it, and a very tiny bit of the steel globe was removed by the friction of the bird's wing rubbing against the steel globe. The bird continued returning once a year. When the solid steel ball of the earth is worn down to the size of a metal BB, that would be the end of the first day of eternity. I must have been speechless! But I knew that it could not be true.

Later, I asked Brother Alexis, "What is the quickest way to get into heaven?" He said that if you died in service to the Lord, as soon as your heart stopped beating, your soul would be in heaven. I didn't believe some of this, though I did think about becoming a missionary and getting killed in Africa. I thought that I'd get right into heaven, and not take the chance of dying with a mortal sin on my soul, and burning in hell for eternity.

I remember one day a Brother asked me if I would run an errand for him after school. I said yes, and after school I walked across the street to the Brothers' house. Brother Alexis came to the door, gave me money and a list of food items to buy. When I returned with the groceries, he gave me a few coins, and invited me to come down inside for a brief visit. I could see that the Brothers were not wearing their habits. They were wearing regular clothes, and some were walking around in their underwear. Feeling uncomfortable, I declined. I was pretty sure that they knew that I lived in a fatherless home.

Mom's Gone…. Dad's Gone

Aunt Mary was Mom's younger sister. Sometimes she would travel by subway from Queens to visit us. She and Mom would sit at the kitchen table, smoke cigarettes, and talk about "L", which was short for Lawrence, my father. One morning, Aunt Mary and Uncle Walter surprised us by showing up at our apartment. Unk explained that he had been 'drafted'. Then off he went carrying a duffel bag. Aunt Mary started crying, so Mom thought it would be a good idea to keep themselves busy with work. As they were washing the large kitchen window, they broke it. Mom wrapped a towel around Aunt Mary's arm, which was bleeding.

Aunt Mary said that it meant "bad luck", but Mom said that was only for broken mirrors. Later they sat at the table and smoked. Mom filled two glasses with wine. Aunt Mary said it tasted bitter. Mom said, "Drink it, and you'll feel better". Hours later, I was in the bathtub. Mom had left the bathroom door open to keep an eye on me. Then the kitchen door opened, and Unk walked in. He said that the army didn't want him because he had failed an examination. He was completely blind in one eye. He had forgotten about it because it had happened years ago, when he was a child cracking coal. A shard of coal pierced his eyeball.

Once, Aunt Mary came to our apartment, and asked Mom if she could take me and Artie swimming. Mom said, "Okay, but they don't have bathing suits". We had never been swimming before. Mom told me that I could use my regular short pants as a bathing suit, and Aunt Mary said, "Let's make a bathing suit for Artie with some cloth". I watched as Mom cut a pattern out, and Aunt Mary began sewing. Presto! We were ready to go. Mom had to stay home with baby, Loretta. Aunt Mary took us to the Coney Island Beach. We had fun running in the deep sand and into the water. Artie looked funny when he came out of the water in his homemade bathing suit. We both got very sunburned.

Getting Food

One day after Mom had gone away (mental hospital), Dad had taken Loretta to live with Aunt Mary and Uncle Walter, he came home with two bags of groceries. Then he didn't come home for several days. When he did, he brought more bags of food, but then he didn't return. We waited every day to hear Dad's footsteps coming down the hall.

Artie and I lived alone in our apartment for about two months. We ate all the food in the apartment. I remember Artie sticking his finger inside an empty mustard jar, trying to get the last bit out. Once, Artie and I bought a big can of dog food. We didn't like the taste, but we finished eating all of it. One day, we went to Mr. Rolo's grocery store, and Artie asked him if we could buy some food, 'on the cuff'. Mr. Rolo told us that our bill was too high already, and that Mom or Dad should come, and talk to him. Artie and I found some food stuff out back in Mr. Rolo's garbage cans. We found better food in the cans that were behind coffee shops and restaurants. At times, I'd look through the baker's window, so I would know when he had finished putting a loaf of bread through the cutting machine. When he had, I would dart in and grab the ends of the loaf that were left in the cutter, and run out.

Sometimes I would follow the fruit peddler's wagon. When he was taking care of customers on the sidewalk side of the wagon, I would take fruit and string beans from the street side of the wagon, and run. I knew he would not run after me because he wouldn't want to leave his horse, wagon, and customers behind. But he was on the lookout for me after that. I believed that anyone would steal, if they were really hungry.

Artie thought we should start selling newspapers, so that we could make money to buy food. We asked a newspaper boy where he got his papers. The Brooklyn Eagle plant was in a different neighborhood. But he told us that you had to have at least a dollar to buy even the smallest number of newspapers. We didn't have any money.

Then I got an idea. [journey from brooklyn] The sidewalks near some subway stations had built-in steel grates that people walked on. I could see coins at the bottom of the grates. When people took money out of their pockets, sometimes a coin would accidentally fall through the grates and down to the bottom. The grates were about 30' long, 8' wide on the surface, and 10' deep. (see photo)

Artie searched our apartment for a jar of Vaseline. I went into Mr. Yourga's workshop, where I found a padlock that looked like it was the right size, and a ball of string. We had never seen anyone fishing for coins, but we went to a busy subway station to see if my idea would work. We tied the string to the padlock and checked that the lock would fit through the openings in the grate. Then we put Vaseline on the bottom of the padlock. When we pulled it up, it had dirt and junk on it, but no coin. So, we wouldn't waste Vaseline, I lowered the dry padlock down several openings in the grate, to line it up over a coin. Then I put Vaseline on the lock and tried it, but the coin fell off before I pulled it all the way up. I learned that it worked better with less Vaseline on the bottom of the lock. Ready, set, go. I lowered the padlock right on it, slowly pulled the lock up, and eased it through the grate. Wow! I had quarter in my hand. We "fished" all day at about five different grates. People would stop and watch us. They had never seen kids on their knees fishing for coins. We fished until it was getting dark. Then we counted the money. We had almost two dollars! However, I realized that we were fishing our way into poverty because soon we would have fished all the grates in Greenpoint.

The next day, we went to the Brooklyn Eagle's newspaper plant, and bought as many newspapers as we could. I sold papers on the corner where the Greenpoint Savings Bank was located. Artie took his papers to the busy Greenpoint Avenue subway station. We were in the newspaper business. I yelled, "Paper, paper, extra, extra, read all about it". I had heard newspaper boys yelling this in the newsreels. I did not understand what it meant, but it helped me sell my papers fast. A couple of men asked me what the 'big extra' was. I faked it, replying "You have to read the newspaper".

Sometimes in the headlines, I saw, HST. I did not know how to read, so I asked Artie what HST was, and he told me that it was for President Harry S. Truman. I started yelling, "President Truman did it." By the second week, we bought about three times as many newspapers. We would go to Rolo's and buy bread, baloney, peanut butter, and milk. If we didn't have enough money, Mr. Rolo would let us buy four slices of bread and a few slices of plain baloney.

[Flash Forward to August 2017: My wife and I were in Manhattan, and I took her to Greenpoint. We found the subway grates. I got down on my knees. Sure enough, there were coins down there.(see photo) I told her that I had started a bank account at Greenpoint Savings Bank, but when things got crazy at home, I never withdrew my money. She wanted to go into the bank and inquire about my two dollars, but I reminded her that we had just paid $740 for our room the night before at the Plaza Hotel and had enjoyed a $115.00 breakfast.]

Locked Out of Our Home

One day, Artie and I came home after selling our newspapers, but there was a padlock on our door. Mr. Yourga had apparently done this. I knew that the only unlocked window into our apartment was a small one over the bathtub in the back of the building. Being smaller, I climbed up a ladder, opened the window, and was able to get inside. I dropped down into the bathtub. Then I unlocked the kitchen window, and Artie climbed in.

A few days later, Artie and I were on our front stoop when a lady came up the steps and asked us what our names were, and if our mother or father was home. Artie told her that Mom got sick, and had to go away. He told her that Dad worked on ships and sometimes was away all night, but that he thought Dad would be home that night. Then she asked me what I ate for breakfast. I told her that I had cereal, eggs, and toast. She wrote our answers in her folder and left. After she left, Artie asked, "Why did you tell her that you ate all that food for breakfast"? I replied, "Why did you tell her that Dad would be coming home tonight"? He said that he didn't lie because Dad might come home tonight! He didn't come home.

Soon after that, Mr. Yourga came into our apartment. A man in a suit and a tie was with him. The man asked us questions. Artie said, "Dad's away at work, and Mom is in the hospital". He asked us what we had to eat, as he looked inside the icebox and opened some of the cupboards which were empty. Then he told Mr. Yourga that he would take us somewhere else to live, because we were too young to be living on our own.

He took us to Mr. and Mrs. Frantangelo's apartment, who lived in our neighborhood. He talked to the woman and gave her some papers. He showed her how to put check marks on the paper for our meals, sleep, and school. After a few weeks, Mr. Frantangelo told us that we couldn't live there anymore, but that he would help us find another home. He took us to a house on Java Street. It sounded like he knew the people who lived there. He gave the man the papers and explained how they would be paid by the City. I cannot recall the family's name, but I recognized the daughter. During the previous summer, I had decided to 'play doctor'. My office was behind Rolo's store. The space had a solid wood fence with a door. I started seeing girls who came into my office for 'examinations'. It went well until one of the girls told her mother, how I used a popsicle stick to examine her. Word spread quickly around the neighborhood. When the lady realized who I was, she booted me and Artie out.

Sleeping in Church

We tried, but could not find a family who would take us in. I got the idea that we could sleep secretly in St. Anthony's Church. And it worked out pretty good. But then Artie and I had a big disagreement. I had gotten into the habit of taking some coins out of the poor box. In the 1940's, a kid could feed himself for about 35 cents a day. A hot fishcake cost $.10, a baloney sandwich was
$.05, and a coke was also $.05. He told me to stop, or I would have a mortal sin on my soul. We agreed to separate. I knew there were plenty of churches in Brooklyn, so I told Artie that he could stay at St. Anthony's. I wandered around looking for churches. I found several, and would change churches frequently. It was getting into the winter, so I bought myself a good warm coat for $.15 in the Catholic Charities Store.

New Homes

I tried to find another family to take me in, but didn't have any luck. I wondered if they knew about by bad reputation, or maybe it was because I was smelly and had lice in my hair? Then I remembered that a few times, Mom would visit a Russian lady who had two daughters on Lorimer Street. I found the building. The lady remembered Mom. I told her that Mom had gotten sick, and had to go away. I told her that my Dad had not been home in a long time, and that the landlord had locked me out. She took me in, made me take a bath, and cut my hair. Then she rubbed some kerosene into my hair, and washed it out in the kitchen sink. Living there was good. But I don't think the father liked me being in their apartment. One day, he gave me my knapsack, and said that I should ask the Brothers at school to find me a home.

I did not go to school. Instead, I went looking for a different church. I went to Dupont St. where I saw a woman with a pail and a brush, scrubbing steps. I went over and asked her if I could help scrub the steps. She asked "Are you looking for money? Where do you live? Where does your father work? What about your mother? Do you have any brothers or sisters?" I told her that I slept in churches. She took me inside, and said that her husband, Abe, would be home soon and that we would talk. They lived in a small dark basement apartment. She told me that her husband worked in a store as a cigar-roller.

When her husband came home, he asked me more of the same questions. Then they talked in a foreign language. When they finished, Mr. Abe said, "This will be your home". He also said, "We have rules. We are Jews." "Do you have any belongings, clothes, or books?"

I said that all that I had is in my knapsack. We ate supper. I slept in the living room on a blanket. The next morning, Mrs. Abe walked me to school. As we got close, she said that she would talk to the principal. She pointed to a spot, and said that she would meet me there after school. Later while walking home, she asked me about school. When we passed the Catholic Charities Store, I told her that's where I bought my coat. She said, "Let's go in and see what we can find for you". We picked out pants, underwear, and socks. When her husband came home, he set up an army cot in the living room for me to sleep on. I wondered where Artie was living, and how he was getting food. My guess was that the Brothers were taking care of him.

Dad's Home - Mom's Home

About a month or two later, Artie found me during recess. He told me that Dad had come to the school the day before, and said that he was bringing Mom home in a few days. After school, I returned to where I had been living. When Mr. Abe came home from work, I explained what Artie had told me. It felt like good-bad news to me. We decided to wait a few days to see if it really was true. During recess, I asked Artie if he was living at home. He said, "Yes, and Dad wants you to come home". I told Mr. Abe about the news. After supper, I packed my knapsack, and the three of us walked to my real home. They talked to my father, and asked about my mother. Then they shook hands. Mr. Abe told Dad that if it ever became necessary, he should bring me to stay with them.

Dad told us that he had gotten a job at the Liberty Dry Dock. On Saturday, he brought Mom home. She hugged us, and cried. She said that we would go to Aunt Mary's, and bring Loretta home the next day. All this was happening so fast; it was like having a dream. But sure enough, the next day, we went to Aunt Mary's, and Loretta came home with us.

Failing First Grade

I was sitting with my classmates when the principal, Brother Irenaeus, entered the classroom. We all stood up. He asked us to be seated. Then he asked me to stand up. I wondered what the heck this was all about. I was not in any trouble. Then he spoke very seriously.

He told the class that I was not being promoted to second grade. As I stood by my desk and listened, he explained that I had not learned how to read, didn't know my script, and got lost while going home after school. He told me to be seated. Then he told us to have a good summer, and to remember mass on Sundays. I was embarrassed. No one said anything to me. I thought, Am I the dumbest kid in the room? This experience had a lifelong impact on me.

I met up with Artie on the walk home. I told him I didn't get promoted to second grade. I wondered if the Brothers knew how many different homes I had lived in while I was in first grade. I told Mom, and she said everything would be okay. When Dad came home, he got very mad, and started cursing the Brothers "in their skirts". I think he wanted to go up to the school, but Mom calmed him down.

Summer in the Streets

There was always activity on the sidewalks and in the street. There were 'walking peddlers' who would walk around the block yelling, "knives…scissors… sharpened…umbrellas repaired". My buddies and I used to sneak up behind the scrap peddler, and pull metal from the back of his wagon. When we had a good pile, we would take it to a scrap-metal yard. The man would separate the copper from the iron and brass, weigh each pile, and pay us. Stealing from the ragman was fun. My friend and I would grab rags off the back of his wagon, stuff them into our sacks, and sell his own rags back to him a week or two later.

Nearby on Provost Street, there was a very large Navy storage place. We could see thousands of gray rafts stacked about 50' high. The hard part was climbing up the rafts, and then squeezing our arms in between them. Inside, we found metal containers filled with chocolate bars, rations in tiny cans. We took the chocolate bars. In one raft, I found a gadget, and took it. I did not know what it was. The next day as I was fiddling with it in our backyard, I pulled on a metal ring, and it blew up! Clouds of orange smoke went up the back of our building all the way to the rooftop. What was worse, it left an orange-colored stain on the back of our building and on the concrete in the backyard. This caused a big commotion. Everyone suspected me. Mr. Yourga questioned me so forcefully that I thought his eyeballs might pop out. Dad was home. He said it looked like someone had set off an emergency signal bomb.

Then summer came to an end, and it was time for me to go back to school. I applied to be an altar boy. When I was not accepted, being disappointed, I went to Brother Irenaeus's office, and asked him why they would not let me become an altar boy. He said that it had to do with the way I looked, shoes with holes and soles flapping. Some students would tease me about my flappers. So, I put rubber bands around both shoes, but they broke before I got to school. After that, I waited and put the rubber bands on when I got inside the school. That worked.

One day, my teacher told me that the principal wanted to speak to me. When I entered, Brother Irenaeus asked me if I had taken Andrew's lunch. I said, "no", and suggested that Andy sometimes leaves his lunch on the curb, and runs off playing ring-a-levio, maybe the street dogs ate his lunch. Brother Irenaeus looked at me as if I was the 'street dog', and sent me back to class. Mom never gave us a lunch for school.

Sometimes Mom would receive a booklet of raffle tickets in the mail. We called them 'chances'. She showed me how to write the buyer's name and address on the stub. The best place to sell 'chances' was to go down into the subway station, and catch people waiting for their train. The bad thing was that I never sold a winning ticket. They never had a chance to win. Mom would throw the booklet of stubs out, and buy food with the money. I knew that this was wrong.

Dad came back home, and got a job with the Circle Line— boats that take people for a ride around Manhattan Island. His job was to catch the rope and tie the boats up when they returned to the dock. I don't think he made much money. He quit that job when he got a better job, unloading cargo from ships. Once when he came home from work, he pulled out a large salami from under his jacket. Later he got a job as a marine machinist. I could tell he liked that kind of work. He treated his box of tools like jewelry. I watched him cover the kitchen table with a large rag. Then he cleaned and wiped each tool down with oil. Several times when he could not find work, he would put his toolbox on his shoulder, and go to the hock shop. The man would give him money for his tools. It probably bothered him when he had to do this.

Dad would send me to a store over on Kent Street, where a man would sell me loose cigarettes and beer. Mr. Rolo wouldn't sell us cigarettes or beer. Artie wouldn't go because of the Kent Street gang. These guys would chase us, and then Dad would get mad if we came home without the beer and cigarettes. I had found a BB gun in a garbage can. It didn't have the wood stock, but I fixed it, tried it out, and it worked. One day, Dad gave me the cloth bag, and sent me to go get him beer and a pouch of Bugler tobacco so he could roll his own cigarettes. I put the BB gun inside the bag and went over to Kent Street. Sure enough, the guys started crossing the street and came at me. I took the gun out, aimed over their heads, and started pulling the lever. They turned and ran. I kept shooting. Pop! Pop! Pop! I aimed at their backs. After that, when I went to the store with the bag, they just watched me from their stoop.

We All Pitched In

One day, Dad left with his toolbox, and didn't come home. By this time, I had figured out that when he left with his toolbox, we probably would not see him for a long time. After a week or two, Mom ran out of money, and she began making flowers out of crepe paper. She bought packets of different colored crepe paper. I watched her as she cut petals out, curled them with a blade of the scissors, and attached them to a wire stem. Then she wrapped green crepe paper around the stems. She would give me and Artie a bunch of flowers that we would sell on the Avenue. They were very pretty, and we sold a lot of them. But I don't think Mom was making enough money.

She did her best to keep us nourished. At times she would send me or Artie to the butcher shop to buy a bag of soup bones from which she would make a 'stew' for supper. Potatoes were our most frequent meal. She would make us potato cereal for breakfast, and then maybe add some spices to it, and we had potato stew for supper. We were 'on our own' for lunches.

I remember the time that Mom took us on a four-mile walk to Aunt Mary's home. We stopped at Calvary Cemetery where we saw a 'choke cherry' tree. They were tiny bitter berries, but we ate all that Mom could reach. Later, we saw a man with his hotdog cart. Mom bought one hotdog, and asked the man to put everything on it. Loretta was given the first bite, then I took my bite, followed by Artie. Mom got what little was left. When we finally got to Aunt Mary's, we had baloney sandwiches. Aunt Mary gave Mom a few dollar bills, and we took the subway home.

It was getting close to Christmas. Mom sent us up to the Avenue where men were selling Christmas trees. They let us gather up the twigs and limbs they had cut from the trees. We took them home, and Mom fastened them with wire to a broomstick. It made a pretty good tree. The day before Christmas, two policemen knocked on our door. One of them was my father's brother, Uncle Louis! We had never met him before, but Aunt Eva had told us that her brother was a NYC policeman. The two policemen sort of looked around our apartment. Uncle Louis said they were going up to the Avenue, and would be back. When they returned, they had a real Christmas tree, and two large boxes of all sorts of food. We had a good Christmas without Dad. (Uncle Louis could have done more to be helpful. Most likely, he knew where Dad was living, and Dad may have even asked his brother to 'look in on us' at Christmas.)

[Flash Forward to 1971: The next time I saw Uncle Louis was in the summer of 1971. Aunt Eva had mentioned that Uncle Louis had been driving to Boston to visit his son. He pulled off the road in a snowstorm to sleep. In the morning his fingers and feet were frozen. Artie and I drove to a nursing home on Long Island to visit him. Uncle Louis was sitting up in bed, trying to light a cigarette. His fingers and feet had been amputated. He appreciated the two small bottles of whiskey that we hid in a plant for him.]

We're in the Shoeshine Business

Artie got the idea that we should become shoeshine boys. We went to the fruit store on the Avenue, and the man let us have wooden fruit boxes. We built two solid shoeboxes. We did not know where to buy a shoe last, the metal piece that the men place their foot on when receiving a shine. So we just made simple ones from wood. We bought polish, shoe brushes, and cleaning liquid. Mom cut some rags up for us to buff the shoes.

I took the corner of Greenpoint and Manhattan Ave. This was a major subway stop. There was a bar and a news stand on the corner. I said, "Shine, mister? Shine?" I did get some customers that day, but mostly, I learned. I had never shined leather shoes. I had to be very careful not to get any polish on the men's socks or the cuffs of their pants. Some men would read the newspaper while I shined; others would talk to me. Sometimes, if it was near the end of the day, I would follow a 'shine', staying on the opposite side of the street. I was curious about where these men who wore suits and neckties lived. I noticed that some of these men went into bars. One day, I asked one of my regular 'shines' if he had ever seen a boy shining in a bar. He said that he never had. I talked to Artie about my idea. He said, "Don't do it". But I decided to try it out. (journey from brooklyn) I got into a few bars, but mostly I heard,

"No shining in here. Get out!" I learned more. In 'beer gardens' men wore work shoes, but in fancy places called saloons or pubs, men wore suits and leather shoes. On my black shoebox, I painted Pub Shine in white letters. Then I planned a route from Oakland St, up Greenpoint Ave, over the Kosciuszko Bridge, and up to Queens Boulevard, where there was an elevated subway. The busiest subway station for people coming from Manhattan was the Queens Plaza station. Whenever I went shining, I carried my shoeshine box in Dad's cloth bag. I also kept a knife in my shoeshine box.

In one pub, a customer said, "Give the kid a chance. I could use a good shine". In a fancy saloon, a guy handed me a dollar bill, as I reached into my pocket for change, he said, "Keep it, kid". When I got outside, I ran right around the corner and out of sight; thinking that he might change his mind and come after me. I knew then that I was on to something good. When a bartender would start to wave me out, I would hold up my box, so he could see that I was a Pub Shine kid. Maybe he would think that other pubs were letting me in to shine.

Later, I refined my route and just did select pubs where I began shining regulars. "Drinkers" were good tippers in these fancier bars. But I still depended on my Queens Plaza post. A couple of times I had to defend my spot from other shoeshine kids, even though this was Queens, and I lived in Brooklyn. The men in suits came down the steps from midtown Manhattan. There was a White Castle restaurant one block away. Sometimes Mom would walk to my post, and I'd empty out my pockets for her. We would have a square hamburger and coke at White Castle. Mom would walk home, and I would keep shining shoes. I had explained to Brother Irenaeus that I wouldn't be coming to school on Fridays, because I had to work so that we could buy food. (journey from brooklyn)

[Flash Forward to August 2017: My wife and I drove my shoeshine route. Approaching Queens Boulevard, I commented that in the 1940s, around the corner on the left, there used to be a White Castle. We made the turn, and there stood the White Castle! The same steps were there, coming down from the subway. It was the exact spot where I had shined shoes seventy years earlier. The odometer indicated that the distance was 2.1 miles from my home!]

After a very long time, Dad came home to live with us again. But soon they started to fight. Mom would yell at Dad, "Go back to your siffed up whores! Don't bring gonorrhea and syphilis back here". We must have heard Mom yell that a dozen times. I didn't know what it meant. I asked Artie why Mom was telling Dad to not come back home, but he didn't know any more than I. A lot of fights ended when Mom would hit Dad with the heel of her shoe— right in the middle of his forehead. He would grab a wet towel, and hold it on his forehead to stop the bleeding. Then he would chase Mom, whipping her with the wet towel, as she locked the door and retreated into the living room. Once he was so angry, he pulled the knob off the door. These were scary fights. Then Dad packed and left again.

One day, I happened to glance up India St, and to my shock, I saw Dad walking down it. But if he was coming home, why was he walking on the wrong side of India Street? I quickly stepped backwards into the alley to watch. I think that he had not noticed me. I was curious because I had noticed a pretty woman in high heels walking down that side several times, and it looked like she had gone into Mrs. Frayer's building. This woman was not from our neighborhood. Dad walked past me, crossed Oakland St, and went into Mrs. Frayer's building. I went to Mrs. Frayer's building. As I peeked through her keyhole, in a mirror on the wall, I saw Dad in bed with the pretty woman. I was beginning to understand why Mom told him to go back to his whores. I wondered if Dad might have been living somewhere in Greenpoint?

Months later, I noticed that Mom had started going out for several hours each day. When she came home, she didn't bring food or anything else with her. So, one day, I watched as she walked to Kent St, crossed Oakland St, and then headed in the direction of Newtown Creek. That was odd, because there were no stores there, or any people who we knew. I ran to the corner of Kent St and peeked around the corner. Mom had just gone into a house. I walked by the house a couple of times, and Mom spotted me. She said it was okay for me to come in. She introduced me to her friend, John. He was a short man, and one of his arms was missing. I felt uncomfortable, but was not completely surprised. Once when I was about to enter our apartment, I saw shadows through the broken glass top of the door. When I peeked through the crack, I was shocked to see Mom sitting on a man's lap in the kitchen, and they seemed to be kissing. I recognized the man. He was from the Italian Social Club on the corner. I backed out quickly, and never told Artie or Loretta what I had seen. But seeing Mom (and Dad) in these situations bothered me.

I remember frequently having terrible toothaches, as my teeth were decaying. Finally, Mom bought a small box of 'piloris pads', which looked like tiny tea bags. I would wedge a bag between my aching tooth and my gum. When I had to swallow the juice, it had a bad taste.

Dad was still gone. But one day, out of nowhere, he stopped me on my way home from school. He asked me to secretly remove a large black photograph album from the bottom drawer of his dresser. He told me to bring it directly to Mrs. Frayer, and leave it with her. I did as he asked. But I thought that this was weird.

Then, all of a sudden, Artie was gone. Mom sat me and Loretta down and told us that Artie quit school, and got a job. Artie was always a little secretive, but I couldn't figure this out. When I asked Mom about his job, she said that she didn't know what his job was, but that he was living where he worked. I looked around the apartment, and his stuff was gone. Artie never returned home to visit, and never sent a letter. Actually, the next time that I saw Artie was at Dad's funeral!

The apartment was getting smelly and dirty. When I would return home at night, the kitchen table would be covered with cockroaches, which would run off the top of the table and hide underneath it. My bed had bugs crawling around, and many times, I woke up in the morning with a cockroach in my ear. To this day, I am repulsed by roaches.

Then Mr. Yourga gave Mom a paper that ordered us to move out of our apartment within thirty days. We didn't have any place to move to, so Mr. Yourga evicted us, and our furniture and belongings were carried out to the sidewalk. Mom had not been paying the rent, electricity, or any bills. Our gas had been shut off for about a year. Someone had put a lock on our electric meter, so we were burning candles. Now things were really bad. But our neighbor, Mrs. Carney, came and told us that the men from the Italian-American Social Club were going all over the neighborhood asking people to donate money for us. Our rent was $17 a month, and Mom had not paid it in months. The men from the Club collected enough money to pay Mr. Yourga all of the back rent. Then they carried our belongings back inside our apartment, and even gave Mom the extra money that was left over.

One day, I was up on Manhattan Avenue, standing with my back to the stores just looking across the Avenue. I had my shoeshine box, but this was not a spot where I had ever shined, and you would never shine in the middle of a block? A trolley was going by. I could hardly believe my eyes. There was Dad looking out the window of the trolley, right at me.

When he saw me, he turned his head forward, and away from me. I ran after the trolley, yelling for Dad. But holding my shoeshine box, I couldn't catch up with the trolley. I think I cried. That was the last time I ever saw my father alive! I know he saw me. I also knew that the trolleys did not cross the water into Manhattan, so Dad must have been living or working in Greenpoint. I had seen him drowning the kittens; in bed with a whore; and other bad things. I didn't like him.

In retrospect, it would have been better if Dad had just stayed away. Having him come home for a couple of months, leave for a year or two and return again (and sleep with Mom) was tough on Mom. I didn't notice any significant change in her from day to day, but it must have been driving her crazy.

It has been said that one of the greatest gifts parents can bestow on their children are moments of their own happiness. My siblings and I never received this gift.

The End

At this point, it is important that readers know the conditions I have described—the physical abuse, the fighting, the hunger, and the stealing happened over a period of ten-years, from about 1942 to 1952. Dad never returned, and Mom always seemed nervous and angry.

Then one day, Mom called me and Loretta into the kitchen, and sat us down at the table. Mom looked at us and calmly said, "I love you, but I have to kill you. Don't be afraid. You are good children, and you will go straight to heaven". Mom stood up, and went to the kitchen counter. I did not have time to think. She took a large knife from the drawer, turned, and faced us. As she took a step toward us, I screamed to Loretta to run to the police station. As Mom came at me with the knife, I somehow managed to get behind her back and tried to hold her arms, but she threw me off. My back slammed into the icebox. The knife fell to the floor, and I ran out. I caught up with Loretta near the top of Java Street. As we turned onto Manhattan Avenue, I looked back and saw Mom running after us with the knife. We ran into a drugstore, and asked the man to help us. He chased us out. We kept running, block.... after block.... after block; screaming for people to help us. Finally, we reached Greenpoint Savings Bank, turned the corner, and ran into the police station.

A policeman was sitting at his desk on top of a platform. "You have to help us. My mother is chasing us with a knife to kill us"! He looked up and said, "What's your name? Where do you live?" I answered, he wrote and asked more questions. I stopped answering his questions, but screamed, "She's going to kill us!" I heard a noise and turned around. Mom had entered the police station, and still had the knife in her hand. Loretta and I jumped down and headed for a door with a red exit sign. I looked back and saw Mom leap over the desk, swinging the knife at the policeman's face. He must have pressed a button because alarms began to blare, and lights were flashing on and off. Loretta and I ran up the steps as policemen came running down. We entered a big room. A policeman took us into his office and closed the door. He tried to talk to us. Loretta was shaking and crying. Loretta never saw Mom ever again!!

The alarms finally stopped ringing. Other police came in. They took us to sit at a long table. A woman sat next to Loretta. There was a policeman on both sides of me and one across the table. I answered their questions. Someone brought in a tray, and gave us blueberry pie and milk. We didn't touch it. Then I heard a different siren coming from outside. Without asking for permission, I stood up and walked over to a window. There was an ambulance parked across the street, and the back doors were open. By now, there were two policemen standing at my side. I saw Mom being rolled across the street on a gurney to the ambulance. She was tied up in a jacket and strapped down. They lifted her into the back of the ambulance, which then drove away with lights flashing and siren blaring.

I learned that Mom had been taken to Bellevue Hospital where she was evaluated, and then transferred to Brooklyn State Hospital for the criminally insane. Mom would spend the next nine years of her life there! Mom was 38 years old when they took her away.

I walked back to the long table, and continued answering their questions. "Was anyone else in the apartment when your mother sat you down? Do you know where your father is? Do you have any relatives in Brooklyn?" A policeman came in and said that they had been to our apartment several times over the years when there had been problems.

(I did visit Mom once in the hospital. We were separated by a thick glass wall. We put our hands on the glass as if we were trying to touch. Mom kissed the glass at the end of the visit. After Mom was released, Artie and I took care of her for the last forty-seven years of her life. Over the years, I was disappointed with Loretta's absolute refusal to visit Mom. She just shut Mom out of her life...no visits.... no phone calls...no birthday cards!)

After a long time, two policemen came in with Aunt Mary. We told her what had happened. She said that the police were going to take us to her home. Aunt Mary and Uncle Walter lived in an upstairs apartment of a private home in Queens. Loretta and I slept in the living room—she on the couch, and I on the floor. After a few days, Aunt Mary took Loretta and me on the subway to Greenpoint, so that we could gather up our belongings. When we got into our apartment, it was obvious that others had already gathered up our belongings. The apartment had been trashed. I did find some of my report cards scattered on the floor. The scene did not surprise me. We knew that the government had taken control of Oakland Street. We had heard that they were going to tear down all the houses and build a highway.

Aunt Mary and Uncle Walter treated us well. Every day when Aunt Mary would hear the door downstairs open, she would pour whiskey into a small glass. As Unk got to the top of the steps, they would kiss, and she would hand him the glass of whiskey.

At the end of the summer, Aunt Mary and Uncle Walt explained that I would not be able to live with them any longer. The owners had complained about the noise, and that we were using too much hot water. Aunt Mary had written a letter to her brother, John, in Pennsylvania. She told him about our situation, and asked if he could take me in. I guess that he wrote back, because Uncle Walter said that I could go there. Otherwise I would have to go to some kind of institution. I said that I'd go to Pennsylvania. (journey from brooklyn) When Uncle John came, he told me that I could live with them until I graduated from high school.

My 'die had been cast' in the crucible of Brooklyn's streets in the 1940s—my survival instincts, my mistrust, and some bad habits. I had learned to live by my wits, and control my destiny as best as I could. I had been damaged. However, I did learn to cope with adversity, and become independent.

My Last Visits with Aunt Mary and Aunt Eva

In 2012, I drove to Port Richie, Florida, and found Aunt Mary living in a nursing home. Unfortunately, she did not recognize me. I showed her photographs of four of her brothers, but she was unresponsive. Then I went back to my car, and found a slightly larger photo of her mother, my Baba. When I placed that photo in her hand, she pulled it close up to her eyes and with emotion, she said, "My mom-ma, My mom-ma". While holding the photo of her mother, Aunt Mary looked up at my face. It was obvious to me that she was trying to figure out who I was that brought this photograph. However, she was unable to go beyond that singular recognition from her past; her "mom-ma". Aunt Mary had a good marriage and had enjoyed life.

Aunt Eva lived with her mother, Nellie, who was completely blind. Aunt Eva had a large 'hope chest' at the foot of her bed. I recall once when Nellie smelled whiskey on Aunt Eva, she said, "You would do better to drink at home". Aunt Eva yelled, "Mind your own business. The boys all ran off to make babies, and I got stuck with you".

After Nellie died, whenever I was in NYC, I would stop to visit Aunt Eva. Once I brought my wife, Eileen, with me. Aunt Eva opened the door, looked at us, and said, "You must be the Jew that he married!" We turned and left. I never saw Aunt Eva again. Artie continued his obligatory visits. One day, he received a phone call from the owner of her apartment. He said that there was something wrong with our aunt. Artie later described to me what he saw when he entered her apartment: "Aunt Eva was sitting slumped over the table with a half-empty bottle of scotch and a cigarette, which had burned to the end, in her fingers. A broken glass was on the floor." Sadly, Aunt Eva never used the items in her 'hope chest'. She lived an unfulfilled life.

During our difficult years in Brooklyn, at times Aunt Eva would surprise us after Sunday Mass, and take us to a bakery for breakfast. Then she would give us some 'spirited advice', and disappear down into the subway. She did this two or three times a year. The last time that Aunt Eva met us after church was on April 13, 1952. She took a photo of Loretta and me dressed in our best Easter clothes. Artie was no longer living with us. (see photo)

Me & Artie Grandpa's Wall 1940   **Me, Same Wall 80 Years later**

Me at Dupont St Park 1942

My Son Mark in Bronx Park 1972

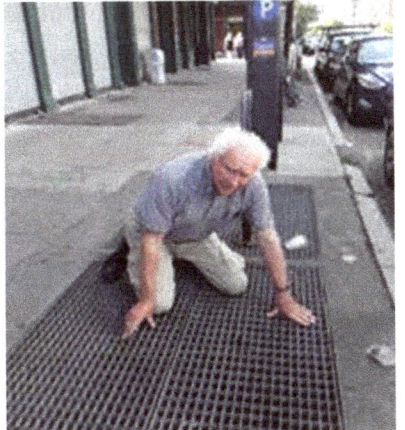
Same Grate I Fished in 75 Years Earlier

Easter Sunday May 13, 1952

St. Anthony of Padua Church

Run for Our Lives May 1952

Chapter 2

FROM BROOKLYN TO THE FARM

Getting to Know My Russian Relatives

Going from the streets of Brooklyn to the countryside in Pennsylvania was a big change. My family lived in the Austin Heights section of Old Forge. The families were Russian, Polish, or Ukrainian. Downtown Old Forge was almost entirely Italian. They controlled most of the businesses, the school board, and the town government. On Mine Street, Aunt Stella and Uncle John lived in the 1204 side of the house. Their son, Junior, lived with them. He was about 20 years old. On the 1202 side of the house, my maternal grandmother, Baba, lived with two of her six sons, Uncle Pete and Uncle Mike (Huggy), and two of her teenage granddaughters (their father, my Uncle Joe, was in prison. Later, he got Mom out of the mental hospital!).

    Uncle Pete was a terrific person. He was a truck driver for a food company. He enjoyed walking over to Andy Butch's house to play cards, and drink in the basement. He married and named his only child, David. I visited him and his family for Russian Christmas in 2017.

    Baba was a hard worker. She fed the chickens and planted the garden. I found it interesting that she received a weekly Russian language newspaper in the mail. She would read articles about Khrushchev and laugh, as she talked in Russian to Aunt Stella. Uncle John was a carpenter. Uncle Huggy worked about three months each year on the bean farms in the Poconos. Later, I would learn that during the War, he had been shipped to Africa. When he returned, he was not the same, and never wanted to get a real job. He was a little odd, but I liked him.

    (In the photos, there is a family picture that Aunt Mary took, and mailed it to Mom at Brooklyn State Hospital. From its tattered condition, I can imagine Mom looking at this picture frequently during her nine years.)

    Aunt Stella was tough, and always had a cigarette in her mouth. She seemed to be the boss on both sides of the house. No one messed with Stella. She took me upstairs and said, "You sleep in this bed with Junior". I didn't particularly like him, and he likely wasn't happy to share his bed with me. Then she told me the rules, and gave me my chores: scrub the outhouse every Saturday, feed the animals, gather eggs in the morning, and crack coal.

I asked questions. "Aunt Stell, where does all the stuff go that drops into the holes in the outhouse?" Junior answered, "He's goofy, Ma." I asked, "Why is this egg different from the other eggs?" Junior replied, "He's goofy." It was a fake egg that was used to urge a chicken to start laying eggs 'or else'. One day, I learned what 'or else' meant. Baba carried a chicken who had stopped laying eggs out to a tree stump, put her foot on the chicken's neck, and cut its head off. The chicken got away, and ran in the yard bleeding until it fell down. That was strange, but so was Baba's reaction. She laughed, and mumbled in Russian.

Country Life

I learned why our dirt road was named Mine Street. Junior and I would take his truck to the mines. We would walk along the railroad tracks filling our burlap bags with big chunks of coal that had fallen off the trains. The bags were heavy, as we carried them to the truck. Once we got home and unloaded all the bags, Junior told me it was my job to crack the coal. It took me about a week to crack it all while screening the coal dust out. Then, I had to shovel it all into the fieldstone coal bin. The only part I did not like was when the shards of coal hit me in the face. I had no goggles, and I remembered how Unk lost his eye!

Junior got drafted and shipped out to Korea. Oh shucks, I thought. Now I'll have to sleep alone in Junior's bed. I heard Aunt Stell ask Uncle John, "J, where's Korea?" He answered that it was near China and Japan. Aunt Stell had never learned to read or write. She baked trays of cookies and pastries with prunes inside. Yep, Uncle John would take boxes of these cookies down to the post office, and mail them to Junior, in Korea.

Uncle John worked at Lockett Lumber in Old Forge. Mr. Lockett also owned a small farm nearby on the Lackawanna River. He allowed Uncle John to keep two cows and six pigs there. My first summer in 1952, I worked on his farm. I didn't like some of the work, like strapping a large metal tank on my back, cranking the handle, and dusting the potato and tomato plants. The white powder would get into my mouth and up my nose. He also had me run through the cornfield to chase the blackbirds out, so he could shoot scatter shots at them. Then I'd gather up these small birds for Mr. Lockett's stew. On those days, I'd go home with red scratches all over my arms and chest from the tough corn leaves. At the end of the summer, Mr. Lockett gave Uncle John fifty dollars to buy me clothes. On my last day there, I stole Mr. Lockett's cabbage knife. It turned out to be the best knife that I have ever owned, and I'm still using it in 2022! I did learn a lot about farming—how to plant vegetables, ride a tractor, dig up potatoes, pull carrots, pick green tomatoes, and save every scrap of food in a swill pail to feed to the hogs. I also learned about cow magnets and salt blocks.

Baba and Aunt Stell did a lot of canning. Down in the cellar, there were long shelves of canned foods: tomatoes, string beans, cherries, plums, and chow-chow. On the earth floor, Uncle John had built large wooden bins. One was for potatoes, one was for cabbage, and another for onions. There was enough food in that cellar to feed everyone all winter long. By spring, the onions and potatoes had tails growing out of them.

[Flash Forward to 2012: My son, Mark, and I went to my Old Forge High School class reunion. We visited the house my grandfather built a hundred years ago. Baba had given birth to eight children in this house without a doctor! The owner let us look around, inside and outside. He was renovating the house. He had torn down the garage, the outhouse, and the barn. He asked me about a rumor. He had heard that a kid had drowned in the outhouse. I told him that it was true. Cousin Theresa had been watching her one year old brother, Charlie, but he wandered off into the outhouse, climbed up onto the wood seat, and fell down the hole. Last year, I found a news item on the internet about this accident.]

When September came, Aunt Stell walked me over the hill to Sibley School. I had brought my report cards with me. She gave them to the principal, Mr. Morgan. He told Aunt Stell that it looked as if I could go to his school and be in eight grade, or go downtown to the high school. Aunt Stell said, "I don't think he's too smart, so he better go here". Mr. Morgan took me into his classroom. It did not take me long to realize what great teachers the Franciscan Brothers were compared to Mr. Morgan. We stayed in his classroom all day, and I started raising my hand in class answering and asking questions. It seemed that sometimes, Mr. Morgan was not too sure of his answers. I'm not certain, but I might have thought that if I answered all the questions, maybe Mr. Morgan would tell Aunt Stell to send me to the high school. One day when I raised my hand to answer a question, he snapped at me, "Put your hand down. We know you're from Brooklyn and know everything". Wow, I never raised my hand again! I did make some friends in eighth grade. To this day, I'm in weekly contact with my eighth-grade buddies, Bulldog (Mike Ezdebski) and Decker (Walter Turowski).

One night, Aunt Stell woke me up when she yelled up the stairs. It was two or three in the morning. Snow had been falling all night. "Davey, come down. Your father is here to see you". We hadn't seen each other in years. I yelled back down, "I have no father. My father is dead". I heard Uncle John tell Dad that he could sleep in the barn until morning. I did not see my father or hear his voice. The next day, I did see his footprints in the snow going from the barn out to Mine Street.

In retrospect, I made a bad decision. I should have talked to him. Later that year, we got word that he had died. Artie got an emergency leave from the Navy. I took a bus from Scranton to N.Y.C., and met Artie and Loretta at Aunt Mary's apartment. At the funeral, I remember Aunt Mary saying, "Somebody better go find a camera and take a picture of 'L' because when Ann gets out, she will never believe that he's dead". He was 53 years of age.

[Flash Forward to August 2018: My son, Mark, located my father's NYC death certificate, which led him to an unmarked gravesite...no headstone...no marker...grown over with grass.]

Back at Aunt Mary's apartment, we spread Dad's possessions out on the floor. Artie, Loretta, and I took turns choosing items. I chose several interesting photographs of the father I never knew. He's all dressed up in fancy clothes. He lived two lives. I believe that these photos were in the black album that Dad had me remove from our apartment and take to Mrs. Frayer's apartment.

Some 50 years later, Artie mentioned to me that he had letters from Dad locked in a metal box. I asked to see them, he said "not now, but someday". I am still trying to gain access to the letters, but no one has been able to find them. The letters would have to have been written in 1952 & 1953. What did Artie know about Dad's other life, that Loretta and I were denied?

Smoking Kielbasy Brooklyn Style

I watched when they slaughtered the hogs. The pig would be hit on the forehead with a heavy hammer. The pig was butchered right there. The various parts were thrown into separate pails. Later, Aunt Stell would fasten a meat grinder to the edge of the kitchen table, and attach a casing to the snout of the grinder. She had already cut up the pork, added a few special pieces of veal, and mixed it all up with some spices. Then she shoved this mixture into the grinder, pressing it down with a wooden plunger. As she turned the handle on the grinder, the meat was forced down into the long casing. When the casing was full, she removed it from the grinder, formed a ring, and tied the two ends together.

Uncle John showed me how to smoke kielbasy. There was a trench about 8 feet long and 10 inches deep. At each end of this trench, a round hole had been dug. We placed a sheet of corrugated metal over the trench from one hole to the other, and put an oak barrel on the top of one hole. A steel rod was put through the sides of the barrel. The rings of kielbasy were hung on the rod inside the barrel. A burlap bag was put over the top of the barrel.

Uncle John explained "Davey, you put some sticks in the big hole. Then you get those logs—from the apple and cherry trees, and put them on top. Next, you put as many rings of kielbasy on the steel rod, so they hang from end to end. Then, cover the top of the barrel with the burlap. Have a pail of water next to the barrel. When it's set up that way, you light the fire at the other end. As the logs burn, the smoke goes through the tunnel, and up into the barrel. Keep the smoke trapped in the barrel by sprinkling water on top of the burlap, and sprinkle water on the logs so that more smoke goes into the tunnel. Aunt Stell will tell you when they are smoked enough".

The next day, Aunt Stella gave me a pail of raw kielbasy. I put them on the steel rod and covered the barrel with burlap. Then I lit the fire—so far, so good. I sat on a stump and sprinkled water. Then, hearing the sound of a basketball bouncing off the metal backboard at Sibley School, I wanted to run over the hill and get into the game. I knew that Junior had thrown old tires behind the barn. I remembered that when we burned tires in Brooklyn, it made lots of smoke. Without thinking, I grabbed a tire and put it on top. Soon the clouds of black smoke went up into the air, through the tunnel, and up into the barrel.

I think Baba saw the black smoke, and told Aunt Stell who came running down the porch steps screaming at me. She grabbed the pail of water and threw it on the fire. Pulling the burlap off the barrel, she said, "Look, just look at what you did!" The kielbasy were black. The casings had burst open. I was speechless. Aunt Stell was not. She cursed at me in Russian. Then she said that all the kielbasy were ruined. "All my time … the pigs…the meat," she went on and on. When she stopped, she marched me up to the porch and told me to take my pants off. Then she poured a pail of ashes and rice on the ground. "Kneel down and don't get up until Uncle John gets home". When he got home, Baba came out and spoke to him in Russian. Uncle Huggy gave him a bottle of beer and whiskey. He downed the whiskey and lit a cigarette. "All right, Davey, get up", he said. "Was that the first batch of kielbasy?" I answered, "Yeah, it was the first". I felt so much better when I realized that there was still a lot of kielbasy in the house. What a relief!

No More Religion

About this time, I broke from religion. It had been building in me for some time. In Brooklyn, I had prayed frequently, asking God to help with our difficult conditions. He never answered any of my prayers. I had always doubted Brother Cipriani's definition of eternity. In Austin Heights, going to confession became a bad experience. The Brothers had taught us that even having 'impure thoughts' in our heads was a sin, that had to be confessed. Now that I was a teenager, whenever I saw a pretty girl, I would have impure thoughts, and had to confess them to the priest. Father Stanislaw usually made it more uncomfortable by asking me questions about what I was thinking. The questions did not feel right to me. His questions became so embarrassing that I started lying to him. Walking home from confession, I thought, This is very bad. I'm lying in the confessional booth. My regular sins can't even be forgiven, and I'm committing more sins by lying. I stopped going to church. When Aunt Stell asked me why I wasn't going to church, I told her I didn't believe in God anymore. [Flash Forward to 1961: My wife, Janet, and I joined the Belvidere Methodist Church. I took an active part by becoming an usher. On World Order Sunday, I spoke from the pulpit. My father-in-law was among the congregants. I saved a newspaper clipping, the title of my sermon was "The Importance of World Law." At age twenty-two, it is likely that I knew very little about what I was preaching.]

Depending on my wives' religion, I've participated in various religions. I have always taken things literally (starting with 'shake a leg'). As such, I eschew unprovable hypotheses, be they supernatural beings or eternal life. To me, these commonly accepted beliefs hold no resonance.

Breaking Bad

To this day, I cannot understand my behavior during the next four years. Aunt Stell had lots of names for me. I was a hooligan, a Brooklyn bum, but mostly a tsyganskiy (Russian for gypsy). She would say, "He's like horse shit—all over the place". I did wander all over the place, just as I had done in Brooklyn. I had developed bad habits: fighting, stealing, and smoking o.p.b's (other peoples' butts) from the street.

I should not have been this way because I had a good life now. I just had to get used to their different ways, such as taking a bath once a week in the summer (once a month in the winter). Aunt Stell would heat up several large pots of water on the kitchen stove and then pour them into a metal tub in the kitchen. She would take her bath while we sat out on the back porch. Then she would call Uncle John in for his bath. When he was finished, he would call Junior in for his. I was the last person in the tub. By then, the water had cooled and really wasn't clean, but I knew my position.

The outhouse was an adjustment. It was a wooden seat with one large hole and one smaller hole in it. We always kept a box of newspapers on the floor.

Whenever we had 'company' on a Sunday, Aunt Stell would give me a roll of toilet paper to put in the outhouse. One of my chores was to scrub the outhouse every Saturday. I didn't like this job. I always thought about little Charlie falling down that hole.

My first week in high school, I decided it was stupid to carry all the textbooks back and forth to school every day, so I stole a second set of books from my classmates. Very quickly, I had a set of books at home to do my homework, and another set in my homeroom desk. It was a great idea, which I used during my four years in high school.

I did get in a lot of trouble in high school…stealing, fighting, and playing hooky. Mr. Fabbo was the principal. We called him Tuffy Fabbo because he wasn't tough at all. One year, I spent two periods a day in his office. Mostly, he would roll back in his chair, and spit tobacco juice out the window. Sometimes he would give me money, send me up to Belladonna's for coffee and a donut, and tell me to get something for myself. I think he liked me.

I played hooky from school a lot, especially when Delford's mother allowed him to drive her car to school. One day, we played hooky and drove to Scranton. We went into Westside High School, and got into a tussle with guys who we didn't even know. On the way back to Old Forge, we stopped at a small store to play the pinball machine. We got into a fight with two guys who were waiting behind us to play the machine. We managed to break a glass door. The owner kept us there until a policeman came. He asked us where we were from, and then started writing our names on a pad, Delford Gatz, Tommy Zupko, William Connelly. The next day, I was sitting up on the bleachers in gym class. The gym door opened, and in walked Mr. Fabbo with a policeman. They walked right over to where I was sitting. The policeman looked up and said, "That's William Connelly". Mr. Fabbo said, "Garrahan, get down here!" He suspended me from school. We had to chip in, and pay for the glass door.

Another time, Bulldog [Mike Ezdebski] and I were getting poor grades in French. I had noticed that Mrs. Kowalchick, our French teacher, used a pencil to write our test grades in a black book. She always put the book in her desk drawer. One night, Bulldog and I went down to the high school. He stood on the ground under the classroom's window and boosted me up. I had unlocked the window during the day, so I was able to get in. I found her record book and pencil, and erased the bad grades and wrote in mostly B's. We passed, but did not learn French.

Camp St. Andrew

Whenever we played hooky, I would come up with a bogus excuse for being absent. When we went to Pittston, I spotted an unemployment office. Bulldog and I went in, thinking we could get a piece of paper with an official agency name on it, to use as an excuse for our absence. However, we actually got jobs working at Camp St. Andrew in Tunkhannock! Catholic seminarians ran the Camp. Bulldog and I found that it was easy to fool the seminarians.

We started working there a week before the camp opened. Mr. Riccio took us to our cabin. He gave us our first assignment, which was to get the kitchen, cafeteria, and canteen ready for opening day. I laughed when Bulldog stole two white chef's outfits. He thought I was stupid when I filled my pockets with play money – the campers were required to exchange their real money that their parents had given them for this play money. They used the play money to buy items at the canteen. I also started buying stuff at the canteen with my play money.

It was not long before Bulldog and I got into trouble. We walked out of camp one night with Bob Zamboni, a camp employee. On a country road, we found a bar, and went in for a few beers. On the way out, Zamboni kicked the screen door open, knocking it off its bottom hinge. We ran. The next morning, a state trooper showed up at the camp with the owner of the bar. We had to pay for the door, and go to confession. We were pissed at Zamboni for involving us.

Some nights, we played poker for money in our cabin. I had marked the deck. Zamboni had a lot of money. When he ran out of money, he said his fancy leather belt was worth five dollars. I gave him $5 for the belt, and then won the money back. I wore that belt for years.

St. Andrew's was a good experience. To swim in the lake, we had to pass a test. I told the lifeguard that I knew how to swim. When it was my turn, I jumped into the lake and paddled out, around, and back. Just as I got close to the dock, the lifeguard yelled, "Stop swimming". I did not know how to tread water. He saw me splashing around, and pulled me out. I had to take swimming lessons with the 6 and 7 year old kids. "Bend… extend…whip…. glide", the instructor shouted repeatedly, as we went through the motions on the dock. I learned to swim!

Every Wednesday night was 'raid night'. The cabins would raid each other, taking items which were then returned the following morning. Bulldog and I did some raiding of our own. We hid flashlights, knives, and other dumb stuff under our cabin where we had already stashed several cots. After that, apparently the seminarians noticed that I was spending play money that I had not exchanged for with real money. They became suspicious, and found our booty under the cabin. I took the rap, and got the boot. Mr. Riccio was at the camp the day I was fired, and I asked him if he would give me a ride to Scranton where he owned a restaurant.

He told me that he had to deliver produce to the Mt. Airy Lodge, and I could ride with him. As we approached the Lodge, he said that he could probably get me a job in the kitchen. He did; and I became a dishwasher. One of the waiters asked me what room I was in. When I told him that I had not been assigned to a room, he offered to share his large room with me. That night he got onto his bed, and I made myself comfortable in a lazy-boy type chair. Then he started talking to me about his 'wrestling days', and coaxed me to get on the bed so he could demonstrate Greco-Roman wrestling. As he began to show me the first 'hold', I jumped off the bed; grabbed my duffel bag, but the door was locked. I backed up, and kicked out the wood louvers.... as he screamed at me to "calm down". I stepped through the shattered louvers; ran out of the building, down to the highway, and hitched a ride to Old Forge. (journey from brooklyn) My uncles, Pete and Adam, were getting ready to drive up to the Poconos to pick beans on the farm where Uncle Huggy was a supervisor. They let me join them. It was good money: $.20 for a basket of tomatoes and $.45 for a bushel of string beans. We were coming off lunch break. I had stupidly left an almost full bushel of beans in the row. I saw a worker picking it up. I yelled, "My beans"! He yelled at me in Spanish. I took my cabbage knife out, and signaled for him to put my bushel down. The other pickers watched. If there was going to be a fight, I knew that I'd have to cut him. I took a few steps forward, and he put my beans down.

That night, in the bunkhouse, I took a few swigs as my uncles passed a bottle of whiskey around. I fell asleep on the porch and woke up in a patch of poison ivy. When we got back home, Aunt Stell was mad at Uncle Pete and Uncle Adam. She made some mud-mix, and put 'bopkie leaves' on my poison ivy. Uncle Pete said, "Ah, Stell, you should have seen the way Davey fought that Spic for his beans".

Russian Weddings

One weekend, we went to a wedding. Aunt Stell and Uncle John took me on a long ride to Lopez. I learned that Lemko weddings last for three days. The first day is the wedding and reception day. The second day is spent at the bride's parents' home. The third day is spent at the groom's parents' home. Also, there is a lot of drinking!

At the end of the first night as Uncle John was driving us back to Baba's sister's farm, the back door of the car we were following flew open. Someone was thrown out of the car. We stopped, and got out. I could see that the woman had cuts and scrapes on her legs. The next morning, we learned that she hadn't broken anything, and that she would be okay. However, the second night's celebration ended badly. Sparky crashed his car, and was killed. I listened to people talking about it. Sparky was not a member of our family.

Fired from All Three Jobs

While living with Aunt Stell and Uncle John, I managed to get fired from three jobs. They never knew why I had come home from Camp St. Andrew's two weeks before Bulldog. Uncle John got me my next job. Vinni and Bobby Belcastro operated two businesses in Old Forge. Vinni ran a bar, and next door, his brother, Bobby, ran a pool hall with a bowling alley in the basement. Bobby hired me as a pin-picker in his bowling alley. I was fast, and could pick two lanes at once, jumping back and forth between the lanes. I liked the place because Mr. Belcastro would let us use the pool tables for free while we waited for the bowlers to arrive.

On a Saturday night, a major league tournament was being held, featuring Frankie Clause, an Old Forge resident who was called the 'bowling schoolmaster' in the newspapers. He had bowled a record number of 300 games. I thought I had a good idea to form a union, and call a strike. As the teams were getting ready to throw their practice balls, all the pickers walked out holding strike signs that I had made. Mr. Belcastro came out. I started to explain that the pickers in Scranton earned eleven cents a game, and that we only got nine cents. He said, "Shut up". Then he asked each picker, "Are you on strike?" Each kid answered, "No". Then he told me to get the hell out of here, and that he didn't want to see my face ever again.

Then Uncle John got me a job at the Maxim plant in town. I worked from 4–10 pm, setting up food and coffee on a wagon. Making the urn of coffee and loading up the sandwiches, chips, and cakes was easy work. The men were given fifteen-minute breaks, and I would push my wagon to regular stops where they were gathered. Without permission, I bought a bag of bagels and a few packs of cigarettes, thinking that I could make some money on the side. But I mixed up the money, and was fired.

Uncle John went out of his way to be helpful to me many times. In Brooklyn, we had no money for toothpaste. In fifteen years, my teeth had never been brushed, and they were badly decayed. He sent me to a dental clinic, but it was too late. Dr. Fitzsimmons pulled many of them out. I tried never to smile. Then, Uncle John took me to a dentist who made false teeth for the top front that hooked on to my remaining real teeth. Wow, what a difference they made. I could smile and laugh. I felt so much better.

Big Trouble

One Sunday afternoon, I saw a few of my guys out near the barn. They asked me if they could borrow my guns to scare some guys up at Haddocks in Avoca. I had stolen three guns from a car, and hid them in a shed. Reluctantly, I loaned them the guns, but I told them that if they screwed up, they were to say that they stole the guns from a car.

Monday morning, my friend, Jack Hatala, called me out of algebra class, and told me that my guys had been arrested with guns. Oh, crap! That afternoon's issue of the Scranton Times had a news item: Old Forge Gun Toters Arrested in Avoca. Several days later, a policeman came to the house, and asked me about the guns. Fortunately, Uncle John and Aunt Stell were still at work.

I pretended that I was surprised to hear that someone said they got guns from me. A week later, Bobby Malinowski's lawyer came to the house and said, "Bobby has a record, and he will get sent away unless you admit that they were your guns". I gave him the same answer that I had given to the policeman. Bobby was sent to Camp Hill, a juvenile reformatory. One of the other guys had to join the military. There was a lot of talk in Austin Heights. Even Mr. Babrosky, the butcher, asked me about it. He said, "A lot of people are saying that they were your guns". I held the line. (journey from brooklyn)

Let's Go to Canada

Our Senior Class was going on the class trip. We could not afford it. So, I said to Bulldog, " Let's hitchhike to Canada"! I told Aunt Stell that we were going to camp-out, and fish on the Susquehanna River for a week. We hitchhiked to Canada in one day. We left early in the morning, got on the Penn-Can highway, got a couple of long rides, and walked over the Rainbow Bridge on the first day! We saw the sign, Welcome to Canada, and a man painting a fence. Bulldog talked to the painter in Polish. He cleaned up, and took us to his home. We ate supper with his wife and two children, and then went to sleep on the floor in an empty room. Before we fell asleep, the man came in and said that his wife was afraid of us, and that he would have to search our duffel bags. We had a couple of knives that we let him hold for us. We ate breakfast with them, and said that we were going to look around Niagara Falls, and that we would be back for supper. We never got back. We walked around Niagara Falls, and then hitched a ride. The man who stopped for us said that he owned a racetrack in Toronto. He asked if we would like to go there with him. We agreed, and arrived at his horse racing track. He said hello to people, and paid for our food. We had a good time watching the races.

The following day, a Canadian soldier in uniform gave us a ride. I sat in the front, and could see that Bulldog was searching through the guy's army bag on the back seat. He paid for our supper and then drove us to Buffalo, N.Y. I became suspicious about why he was taking us back to New York without saying anything to us. Then he took us to a lounge where he seemed to know people. We sat in a large booth with plants on both sides. We ordered shots and beers. Suspicious of his motivation, I began pouring my whiskey into the planter. Bulldog kept drinking. Then the soldier said, "It's getting late. I know a hotel nearby". When we got to the hotel parking lot, I told him that we didn't have money for our room. He said he would pay for it. The hotel was a crappy place. I listened as he talked to the man behind the wire mesh. I got the soldier's attention, and reminded him that we wanted a separate room. "Not necessary. It's a large room", he said. The guy behind the wire mesh told us to step outside to resolve our issue.

We went outside, got into the soldier's car, and began to argue. When I called him a "f***in blockhead", he got out and went to the back of the car. I got out and ran. Looking back, I saw that he was holding a tire iron and that Bulldog ,who drank too much, was still in the car. I ran back, and hit the guy in the back. (journey from brooklyn) Bulldog got out, and finished him off pretty good. We left the guy lying there in the parking lot, and walked into downtown Buffalo. The night clerk at a fancy hotel let us sleep in the big chairs in the lobby. In the morning, we decided to head home. The return trip took almost three days! It was a great vacation. When I got home, I told Aunt Stell the truth—that I didn't catch any fish. She never found out about our adventures in Canada.

Graduation Day

Aunt Stell and Uncle John did not come to my graduation. I walked home alone. It was getting dark, as I went up the porch steps with my high school diploma in my hand. Aunt Stell and Uncle John were sitting on a double rocking chair. I noticed that there was a suitcase at the top of the steps. Aunt Stell spoke first, "Davey, we bought you a suitcase for graduation. I packed all your stuff in it". She kissed me goodbye on the cheek. Uncle John stood up, shook my hand, and wished me good luck. I thanked them for taking care of me, took my suitcase, and walked out to Mine Street. Uncle John had kept his word, to let me live with them until I graduated from high school!

I knew that I had caused them trouble, but I wasn't prepared for this. I didn't know what to do; so I walked over the hill to Bulldog's house. As I got close to his house, I heard music, and saw colored lights hanging around the front porch. All of his Ezdebski relatives were there for his graduation party. He spotted me. Walking over, he said, "Hey Dave, what's with the suitcase?" I told him that I was going to New York, and that I needed some money. I tried to sound like this was my plan. "How much?" he asked. Bulldog received a lot of money as graduation gifts. I think he gave me fifteen dollars.

I hitched a ride to Scranton, and bought a bus ticket to New York City. (journey from brooklyn) I checked inside my suitcase to make sure that Aunt Stell had packed my cabbage knife. She did! I thought that I knew NYC, and felt confident. I didn't have any plan. The bus stopped at the Port Authority terminal. It looked kind of creepy. I walked over to Times Square. When I got there, I realized that I did not know this part of New York City. When I lived in Brooklyn, every Fourth of July, the kids in my neighborhood gathered up all of their money, and gave it to me to buy fireworks for them. I would take the subway into Manhattan; walk to Chinatown; and buy all the fireworks for them. I also took 'my cut' of the money. But I didn't know the rest of Manhattan. Times Square was full of honky-tonk joints, hookers and peep shows. I was intimidated by the scene. I walked back to the bus terminal, and tried to figure out my options. I slept on a bench in the terminal.

When I woke up, I took the subway to Brooklyn. My neighborhood had changed in five years. All of the tenements on Oakland St were gone. A four-lane highway, McGuinness Boulevard, replaced Oakland St. I did not know where any of my friends had moved. I wondered what I should do. Maybe I should go to the recruiting office and enlist. But I thought that I could do that at any time. Then I remembered that at Dad's funeral, Artie told me that if I was ever in trouble, I could count on Commodore Perry at the Larchmont Yacht Club, in Larchmont, N.Y. I wasn't in any trouble, but thought that maybe I should try to find this Club. (journey from brooklyn)

I Can Drink Whiskey In The House

Me and Loretta with Russian Relatives

In The Ukraine Alcohol With All Meals

Me and Bulldog At The Reservoir

Bulldog, Me, Decker With Wives, Charlotte & Erika

Chapter 3

FROM FARM TO YACHT CLUB

The Larchmont Yacht Club

[NOTE: From 1957 to 1961, I worked at the Larchmont Yacht Club in New York, and attended East Stroudsburg State Teachers College in Pennsylvania, concurrently.

Shuffling in the text between my experiences at the Club, and those at College would confuse the narrative. Accordingly, I describe my 'club life' in this chapter, and my 'college life' in the following chapter.]

I picked up a road map at a gas station, and found Larchmont on it. It was not far north from NYC. I took a subway train to the end of the line. Then I hitchhiked to Larchmont, and walked to the Larchmont Yacht Club. It was an impressive, elegant club on Long Island Sound.

I walked up to the front desk, and asked where I could find Commodore Perry. The man at the desk asked someone to take me up to the Commodore's room on the third floor. I knocked on his door, and introduced myself. I felt comfortable and relieved to be in his small room. He obviously was not a commodore. He was the club's electrician, and was so well liked by Club members that they had made him an 'Honorary Commodore'. On weekends, he would dress up in his commodore uniform, and direct parking for the members. I explained my situation, and asked if I could work and live there. For a minute, he just looked at me and my suitcase. Then he said he would speak to the manager, Mr. Carney (Robert F. Carney was the older brother of Art Carney, who was on television with Jackie Gleason in The Honeymooners).

Mr. Carney was a tall, distinguished looking man with white hair. He was very formal, stating that most of the yachts had refrigeration on board. He continued, "But they could use a hand getting their suitcases and gear down to the dock. Actually, it might be good having you posted at the icehouse.

Some members still use ice, and now they phone the boatyard when they need someone to cut them a block of ice. You will stay up in the 'monkey house', and take your meals with the help. How long will you need to stay here?" I told him that I did not have any plans. "You better talk to Mr. Perry about that. We don't have much work during the winter". Wow…I was in.

I took my suitcase, and walked up to the monkey house. I immediately saw how the building got its name. Everyone housed there was an immigrant of color. Dimas welcomed me at the door. We sat on his bed and got to know each other a bit. His wife and five children lived in Puerto Rico. He sent them money from his earnings as a busboy. He went home once or twice a year. I mentioned to Dimas that I hadn't had breakfast or lunch, and I was hungry. He said that he was going over to the help's kitchen, and that I could come with him.

[Flash Forward to 1960: By this time, I was out of the monkey house and living with the assistant manager and club members in the main building. And I had bought a car! But I never forgot the guys who had welcomed me into their monkey house home. I treated them to a tour of Manhattan, and a feast in Spanish Harlem. For some,   it was the first time they had ever been served.] (see photograph)

I quickly learned how to cut a 150-pound cake of ice into smaller blocks, and to place them in a wagon. I pushed the wagons down to the dock where I handed the ice off to a launch man, along with the member's other luggage and gear. The launch man took the members and their gear out to their yachts. I would usually receive a dollar tip from each member. Then I learned that I would also receive a regular paycheck from the club. What luck!

At the end of the first week, I mentioned to Mr. Carney that   I had too much 'downtime' between customers, and that I did not like sitting in the icehouse. He gave me a few small painting jobs, which I finished in a day or two. I then suggested to him that the Pandemonium, which had been built in 1902, could use a good painting before it started to crack and peel. I told Mr. Carney that I did not want any extra pay, but that I just liked to work. He looked skeptical, but said, "See Mr. Dempsey. He will set you up with a ladder, a brush, and paint, but keep your eye on the icehouse. I don't want any complaints".

The next day, a long-retired Club employee, Mr. Bill Lynn, who had worked at the Club for 50 years, was dropped off by his daughter at the rear entrance at the back of the garage. Mr. Lynn started at the Club as a 'stable boy', and later worked in the garage. Bill's routine was to sit atop his old wood desk in the garage for about an hour, and then walk down to the icehouse. He would sit there, smoking his pipe while talking to me. Mostly, it was about the 'good old days' when this was a 'yachtsman's club'. Mr. Lynn seemed to think that swimming and tennis were 'distractions'. He cheerfully greeted passing members by name, and at times after they passed, he would share a private comment with me.

Saving Money for College

I had no interest in college. However, when Mr. Carney asked me how long I needed to stay at the Club, I replied that I had no plans. He said that I better talk to Mr. Perry because there was no work during the winter. Speaking with Mr. Perry, he urged me to go to college, explaining that I would have room and board at the college, and then return to the Club in May. That made sense to me, and I wrote a letter to East Stroudsburg State Teachers College. (journey from brooklyn) The school sent me an application and requested a transcript. I returned the completed application along with a letter stating that I would bring them a transcript in September.

Now, I needed to save a lot of money. Mr. Carney told me that I could roll gravel tennis courts and reline them with white powder every morning at 6:30 a.m., and that he would pay me an extra twelve dollars and fifty cents a week.

Several members got to know me at the icehouse. Mrs. Legler was the first to ask me if I would prep her yacht for weekends. I said yes, and charged her seven dollars. Then Mrs. Legler introduced me to her lady friend who had a much larger yacht. I charged her friend fifteen dollars. This was fun for me. After supper, I would row out to their yacht. I would polish all the brass and chrome, clean the refrigerator, sink, and toilet, scrub the galley, and wash the salt off the exterior.

I did not realize that the Norwegian guys in the boatyard had a monopoly on this work. They did not like the fact that I was cutting in, and charging lower fees. I asked Mr. Perry what he thought I should do.

He spoke with Captain Toby. Then Tommy Thompson, the senior launch man, came down to the icehouse to talk with me. He really understood my situation, and talked to me like a friend. I told him that I wouldn't take on any additional yachts. I got to like Tommy and Captain Toby. [Flash Forward to 1965: My wife and I were visiting the 1964/65 World's Fair in Queens, and among the thousands of people, I recognized Capt. Toby, who was not in his Club uniform. Sadly, I learned that Commodore Perry had passed away. I told Capt. Toby about the surprise visit that Mr. Perry had made to my home on the Delaware River in 1962.]

Working Three Jobs

From 1957 to 1961, the Yacht Club was my home. During my Easter vacation in 1958, I sat down with Mr. Carney to discuss my upcoming summer work. In short, I had to convince him that I could do three full-time jobs. (journey from brooklyn) This is how I would do it. I would place a sign above the telephone in the icehouse, which read 'Please Call Beach Grill for Ice Service'. While cleaning tables up on the patio at the grill, I would position myself in front of the beach grill, which was midway between the icehouse and the service dock. Whenever the phone rang in the grill, whoever answered it, would lift his white hat off, if the call was for ice service. I would be at the icehouse within one minute.

While standing outside the grill, I had a clear view of the service dock, and could see when a yacht was coming in for service. I would remove my apron, and get over to the service dock in time to tie up the boat, and provide it with fuel and fresh-water.

I explained to Mr. Carney that the Club did not need these positions as full-time. He knew that the ice boy position was not a full-time job. Likewise, the patio boy at the beach grill had very little to do. Mr. Carney seemed annoyed as he said, "Are you saying that you want all three jobs? What about Billy and Dennis?" I responded that Dennis lived in Larchmont and didn't need the money. Billy did not take his job seriously. He knew that I was a great worker, and that club members liked me. He gave me the three jobs, but warned me, "There must be no complaints". There were no complaints.

Near the end of that summer, I was in my usual position out on the beach grill's patio with my eyes on the service dock when Mr. Attilio, the maitre d' in the dining hall, approached me. He said, "I've been watching how you move among your three jobs. I can use you upstairs". I said that I liked what I was doing, but that I'd think about it. Back in the monkey house, I asked Dimas what his busboy job was like, and how much money he made. We talked. He told me there was a good chance that Mr. Attilio would soon promote him to be a waiter.

A week later, Mr. Attilio came down to the grill, and told me that whenever I stayed at the club during my holidays, I could team alongside Dimas in the dining room, and that I would have regular work all year. I thought: Attilio gets a great worker; Dimas gets the waiter's position he has dreamed of; and we both make more money! (journey from brooklyn)

I'm a Busboy

On Thanksgiving 1958, Norbert, a German waiter, gave me black trousers and a white shirt. Robert, a French waiter, gave me a black bow tie, and Miss. Mandeville, who ran the laundry service, fitted me with two busboy jackets. Attilio prepped me, "No conversation with the members. Interact verbally only as a function of your role butter on this side… never put your arm in front of a member…stand off to the side with your eyes on your tables… remain silent".

I learned quickly. I worked all the holidays during my years attending college. The Larchmont Yacht Club was my home away from my college home.

I knew the head bartender, Gene. I had done him favors like cracking ice and bringing it up to the bar, which was directly above the icehouse, and slicing up lemons, limes, and oranges for him. Sometimes he would ask me to go down to the kitchen, and bring up a couple of trays of clean glasses for him. I was like Gene's unpaid bar boy.

Tom Saunders, assistant bartender, spoke with a raspy voice. He said that he had burned his vocal cords drinking a liquid that had some alcohol content. He was a reformed alcoholic who had lost his job on Wall Street. I asked him, after all that, why he became a bartender? He said it was the safest place to work for a reformed alcoholic. Then Tom dropped a bomb. He said, "Mr. Carney is an alcoholic". He told me that Mr. Carney had also hired men from his AA group to work at the Club.

The following year, Gene was terminally ill in a hospital. He told Mr. Carney that he would like to see me. I went to the hospital. Gene whispered, "I trust you. There's a false bottom in the bar. On Monday when the Club is closed, please remove everything to your car and get rid of it". He also hinted to me that Don, the Quartermaster, probably knew what he had been doing. I did as Gene asked.

Now I'm the Quartermaster

Attilo was not pleased, but Mr. Carney gave me the position of Quartermaster when Don "resigned abruptly". I had padded his receipts. (journey from brooklyn) I served cocktails, carrying my small round tray of drinks out along the veranda that overlooked Larchmont Harbor. I served the special men only room, and a large room inside just off the veranda. I earned more than I did working three jobs.

As pay, I received a percentage of all money made on the liquor I served. I also worked the large parties in the Pandemonium where all of the waiters and I split the percentage. Once, it was necessary to bring in union waiters for a large wedding party. I noticed something odd going on behind the bar. A union waiter was standing behind the bar, hunched over the metal sink. Walking closer, I could see he had a 1.5 liter bottle of champagne turned upside down in each of the sink's four corners with a napkin draped over the top of each bottle. I asked him what he was doing. He said, "This is a hell of an easier way to make money than running around the

Pandemonium topping off champagne glasses". I didn't stop him; but I did have his name removed from the list of approved union waiters for our Club.

Mr. Carney Needs an Assistant Manager

The Larchmont Yacht Club had hosted Race Week since 1885, featuring hundreds of racing boats from distant ports. Race Week ran for nine consecutive days. Reporters from all the major newspapers covered the events. It is difficult for me to describe the hectic atmosphere during those nine days. There were strangers all over the place: at the bar paying cash…in the locker room…on the docks…and in the dining hall.

Mr. Carney asked to speak with me in his office. He seemed a little edgy. He told me that Jay, his assistant manager, had just taken a position at another club. Race Week started next week. "Dave, you know the work that Jay did. Do you know someone who could take his job, fast?" I really didn't, but I told him that the only person who could do it was my friend, Guzzi. (journey from brooklyn) He and I had completed a big job in college. I said, "he's smart, honest, and very organized".

Mr. Carney called Mr. Harley, the switchboard operator, into the office and told him to find Dominic Guzzi in Old Forge, Pa. Soon Mr. Harley said, "I have Mr. Guzzi on the line". Mr. Carney asked him to put the call through to his office. He told me, "Dave, talk to your friend about the job. When you're finished, hold the line open and open the door".

"Guz, are you working? That's great. Listen. Mr. Carney, Art Carney's brother, needs an assistant manager real quick". Guzzi replied, "Are you kidding? The only boat I've ever been on was a canoe, and that did not end well". I told Guz that I knew the club and Mr. Carney 'inside out.' I said, "I'll help you. You can do it. Talk to Mr. Carney". When the call was over, Mr. Carney said, "He's never managed anything, but he sounds intelligent, he speaks well, and he's not working. He'll be here tomorrow afternoon for an interview".

Out of the Monkey House

Never could I have imagined the lifelong bond that would develop between Guzzi and Mr. Carney. Guz had studied to become a priest. Mr. Carney was a devout Catholic. Later they would pray together. Guz knew where to look for Mr. Carney whenever he 'fell off the wagon'. This was a great match for everyone. Mr. Guzzi was given Jay's large room in the main clubhouse. I suggested to Mr. Carney that if I lived in Guzzi's room, I could easily brief him on who was who, and what was what. He agreed. I was out of the monkey house, and into the clubhouse! (journey from brooklyn) Only Mr. Ogilvy questioned what an ice boy was doing living among club members. I recently Googled Stanley Ogilvy for the correct spelling of his name. I learned that in 1993, Stanley Ogilvy wrote a book entitled, The Larchmont Yacht Club: A History, 1880–1990. Now I can understand why he thought it was improper for me to be living in the club house. In the end, we did survive Race Week! Guzzi visited Mr. Carney throughout his life. Guz died in 2018.

[Flash Forward to 2018: Upon returning from a Lemko Association meeting in Connecticut with my wife and son, we decided to visit the Club. I had not been there since 1961.The monkey-house had been 'repurposed'. Walking down to the icehouse, to the right was the Pandemonium that I had painted in 1957. It had been remodeled and looked great...but I preferred my forest green color. Later, with cocktails, my wife and son were comfortably seated on the veranda overlooking the harbor. While there was an empty chair next to them, and they asked me to come and sit down, I could not get myself to sit there. I had served drinks to Arthur Knapp, Stanley Bell, Rudi Schaefer, Monte-Sano, et.al in these chairs in the very same corner. Many times. During Race Week, John Walhgen, Messalina's owner, we were told, inside the Holy of Holies Club, every year, would climb up to the high diving board, squirt lighter fluid on his entire body, ignite it and dive into the pool.]

Club Officers

Mr. Carney, Capt Toby, Don, Chef Louie, Al, Attilio, Gene (All the bosses posing for the Ice Boy!)

Treating My Monkey-House Friends In Spanish Harlem

Quartermaster Bar 2018

Chapter 4

I'M IN COLLEGE

There were two turning points in my life. Being a college student coincided with my four years working at the Larchmont Yacht Club. Both were learning experiences in different ways. Both were transformative, and both gave new direction to my life. Still controlling my destiny.

All my relatives were working-class people. None had gone beyond grade school. I expected college to be very difficult. I had never read a book in my life. There were no books in our apartment in Brooklyn, or in Aunt Stella's home(she never learned to read). I had never been in a library. So I was entering a new world… just as I had entered a new world at the Yacht Club three months previously!

I had confidence in myself. I had a few excellent teachers at Old Forge High School, including Mrs. Wozniak, who took chewing gum from my mouth, rubbed it in my hair, and slapped my face, so that she could teach me English. Knowing that I liked mathematics, she explained that every word in a sentence has a function. In math each number and symbol in an equation has a function. She taught me to diagram compound-complex sentences, likening them to equations.

[Flash Forward to 1975: After I delivered the commencement address to the graduating class of Old Forge High School, Mrs. Wozniak approached me and said, "Congratulations! You were the smartest troublemaker in all my years of teaching".]

Remedial English, Remedial Math, and the Speech Clinic

I decided to have a double major, mathematics and physical science, with a minor in social studies. For some reason, the college put me in remedial math and remedial English. I was also required to attend the speech laboratory. I went to the speech lab twice a week. Mr. Dunning would put different sized marbles, which had a colored string hanging from each, in my mouth. He would read words from a card, as he tugged on the different strings. I had to pronounce the words properly. I thought that this was a waste of time, but guessed that they had not had any students from Brooklyn. I was aware that I talked with a Brooklyn accent. The guys in the dorm would tease me because I would say 'dees, dem, and dose'... instead of these, them, and those.

There were several very good aspects of college. Going into the cafeteria, and being able to select from so many food choices, and eating as much as I wanted, was great. There were only eight buildings on campus. I was assigned to the new Shawnee dormitory. It was impressive.

But I'm Too Smelly

Students were given clean sheets and towels every week. Each room housed three students who shared one closet. One of my roommates asked to be reassigned during my first month. I asked the other roommate, Larry Hardinger, why Ralph had left. He opened our closet door and said, "Just smell". It did not smell too bad to me, but I got the message. The problem was that I didn't have enough clothes. But I solved that problem. (journey from brooklyn) Students took their dirty clothes to the laundry building. The clothes would be washed, dried, folded, and placed in a cubbyhole that had the student's name on it. I hung around outside the laundry room waiting for a guy to go in without dirty laundry. If he was about my size, I would look to see where his cubbyhole was. The following week, I would take his clothes. When winter arrived, I wrote to Bulldog, and told him I needed a pair of shoes and a winter coat. He brought a good winter coat and a pair of shoes to me at college. I could always count on Bulldog!

Meanwhile, I got a job in town washing dishes, and a job in the college library, which paid seventy-five cents per hour. In my library work, I came across a publication, Writers' Market. It included names of magazines that paid for written articles. I wrote and submitted two articles, both of which were accepted for publication. I do not recall the names of the magazines or the subject of my articles. I do recall the compensation was meager. They paid pennies per word!!

Keeping my eyes open for opportunities to make extra money, I saw an item on a bulletin board. The Pocono Mountain Art Club was seeking a male model. I removed the ad, so that I would eliminate competition. (journey from brooklyn) I wasn't even sure that I wanted to do this. Me, a male model? The art club was located three blocks from the restaurant where I worked three nights a week, and they met on a night when I didn't work. So I became a model. At the end of each night's sitting, they would pass a can around for my pay. Once they were practicing new chalk techniques, and the sitting lasted almost two hours. That night the can had ten dollars in it! One night as I was getting ready to leave, I asked a man, "What happens to all of these sketches of me?" He told me that most of them were probably thrown out. He asked if I would like some? The following week he brought in two sketches, signed and dated. His name was Shorty Widmer. One sketch survived. (see photo)

While reaching up for my East Stroudsburg State Teachers College 1958–1959 catalog to refresh my memory about my college costs, a bookend fell to the floor. As I picked it up, I noticed something on the bottom that surprised me. Written on masking tape, in my handwriting, "ESSTC 1959, I'm Flushed". The bookends had survived sixty years of my moves across the country, and I never noticed this note on the bottom. In 1959, I considered myself to be flushed with money to the point that I could make a nonessential purchase. Later, I bought a slide-rule so that I could compete with my classmates in physics and spherical trigonometry. The instrument came in a leather case which I proudly hung from my belt.

What? I Have to Go Home?

It was Thanksgiving morning of 1957. I walked down from my room. As I passed Dean Martin's office, I heard, "Garrahan, where are you going?" I answered that I was on my way to the cafeteria for breakfast. He said, "It's closed. The college is closed. It's Thanksgiving. Now get going home". Stepping into his doorway, I said, "I don't have a home to go to".

He sat me down, and I explained my situation. I didn't know that colleges closed for holidays, and besides, I had paid all my fees for the first semester, which included room and board. I was shocked. He picked up the phone and called Dean Eiler. He asked Dean Eiler if he and his wife, Betty, were having relatives in for the holidays. The answer was, "Yes, but he can stay here. I'll drive over and pick him up". As I was leaving to wait outside for Dean Eiler, Dean Martin yelled out, "And Garrahan, remember, you better find a place to stay for Christmas, New Years, and Easter".

I knew nothing about college life. I had heard about Harvard and Columbia at the Yacht Club. Soon I learned that ESSTC only prepared students to become teachers, but I had no interest in becoming a teacher! And the College's specialty was preparing students to become physical education teachers. One semester, I took a course, Chemistry of Foods and Nutrition, not realizing that this course had been designed for physical education majors to meet their chemistry requirement. At best, the course would have been appropriate for high school students.

Free False Teeth

Professor Kovarick, my remedial math instructor, told me that I didn't belong in remedial math, and he had me moved into his algebra class. Later, Professor Fritz asked to speak with me after class. He gave me a note to take to the dean of instruction, Francis McGarry, requesting that I be moved into a regular English class. Then he said that it appeared to him that my false teeth did not fit properly. He was right. Several times, I had been embarrassed when my teeth fell out as I was eating in the cafeteria, and students noticed. I had outgrown my false teeth.

He told me that he knew a good 'dental mechanic' who could make me a new set of false teeth that would fit properly. I told him I could not afford the cost. He replied that he would be happy to pay for them. I hesitated because I suspected he might be a homosexual. Then I accepted his offer, knowing that I could handle myself in that situation. (journey from brooklyn) He drove me to the dental office in Washington, New Jersey. The dental mechanic took an impression. A few weeks later, I had my new teeth. They were the right size and color, and fit perfectly. Professor Fritz was just being a very good person!

In January, a sophomore, Janet, asked me to take her to the annual Turn-Around Dance. She told me that this dance was different from all the other school dances. If an upper-class girl asked a freshman boy to this dance, the guy had to accept the invitation. The only dances that I knew were wild Russian polkas, but I accepted. We became friends, however it was obvious to me that her overly strict religious parents did not approve of me. (Subsequently, we married.)

Some Recognition

My physics professor, Dr. George Gessner, made a recommendation to the department that I receive the annual award for achievement in physics. It was a special surprise, especially coming from him. The word on campus was that he had been a member of the team that had worked on the Manhattan Project. The award turned out to be a 580-page, leather-bound book of scientific tables and formulae. My name was embossed in gold on the cover!

People were beginning to know me on campus. I was studying inorganic chemistry, and I really got into it. I wrote a letter to the American Chemical Society to inquire about the possibility of forming a chemistry club on our campus. (destiny control) They mailed me the paperwork, and I became the founding president of a new club on campus, the Atomium Club.

In my junior year, I was inducted into Sigma Zeta Tau, a national honorary science society for third and fourth year students who had reached a high level of achievement in science and mathematics. (see photos)

My Best College Experience: The Proposal

The best experience I had in college did not take place in a classroom. Rather, it was related to my job in the library. I noticed that the library director, Russ Emele, was doing a lot of pacing around, and chain smoking. He seemed edgy and was meeting more frequently with the other librarians. I asked him if something special was going on. He explained to me that the new library building construction was nearing completion. Plans had to be made to move hundreds of thousands of books, magazines, newspaper clippings, artwork, microfilm, microfiche, and slides from the present location into the new library building.

He asked me if I had any ideas?(a few months later, Mr.Carney would ask me if I knew someone to be his assistant manager!) I asked Mr.Emele what kind of plans they were coming up with. He said, "Al wants to put it on the department heads to get their stuff over there, but I can see that getting all screwed up". The library was located in the basement of the girl's dormitory since the college's founding in 1893. Over the years, as the college grew, the library was expanded by using adjoining rooms and various storage areas.

I thought about it as he was talking, and told him that the first step would be to conduct a complete inventory of all the library's holdings, their location, and the shelf space they occupied. Mr. Emele told me that I could use my library work hours to work on this project. I returned to the dormitory, and got my friend, Guzzi, interested. Together, we came up with a detailed plan.

Construction of a building, within fifty feet of the library, had just been completed. Later this structure was incorporated into the new library. We were given permission to use the building as we moved forward with our project planning. We developed eighteen categories of materials to be moved, and color-coded each. The shelves in the new building would have corresponding color-coded labels. Our plan called for student workers using library carts to form a chain from the old building and continuing unbroken into the new building. The movement would continue until all holdings were in place in the new library. Guzzi and I detailed the number of carts required, and made provision for night lighting, rain, and substitute replacement workers.

We reviewed our plan with Mr. Emele. And he scheduled a meeting for Guz and I to present the plan to the entire library staff. At the meeting, there were a lot of 'what if' questions, which we answered. Mr. Emele reviewed the proposal with maintenance personnel and department heads, and submitted it to the Dean. Our plan was approved! (journey from brooklyn)

Big Reward

Mr. Emele saw me as some kind of hero. I received perks. I no longer had to punch my timecard in and out every day. I simply had to write down my total hours, and give them to Mr. Emele at the end of each week. But that was just the beginning. I had no idea that Mr. Emele was president of the Belvidere Board of Education in New Jersey. When Janet graduated, the Belvidere Board of Education appointed her to a second-grade teaching position. Six months later as I approached my graduation, I had already received several offers of employment. It was unusual for a teacher to be certified to teach all the courses within the mathematics, and physical sciences curricula, as well as social studies. Mr. Emele, however, created a unique position for me at Belvidere High School.

Have Car, Can't Drive

It would take me at least six hours to get from the Yacht Club to the College. I had to walk a half-mile from the Club to the train station, and wait for a train to bring me to Grand Central Station. From there, I would walk to the Port Authority bus terminal and wait for a bus to East Stroudsburg. Finally, I would walk a half mile to the college. Every weekend, I would arrive back at college at 7 a.m. on Monday, and ready myself for my 9 a.m. class. And on Fridays, I would reverse the trip, and get to The Club at midnight. I really needed a car.

So, I hitched a ride to Old Forge, and asked Uncle Huggy if he would take me to Moosic Motors to buy a car. I selected a black Pontiac. Then I asked Uncle Huggy if he would drive my car off the lot, and park it on Moosic Road. He wanted to know why? I told him that I did not know how to drive! We left my car on Moosic Road. Uncle Huggy dropped me off at Bulldog's house. Bulldog and I went down and got my car. He drove it up to the top of Bald Mountain, and taught me how to drive in one day! The next day, Sunday, I drove back to college, slowly and very carefully. I've been driving sixty-four years and have never had an accident—not even a fender bender in a parking lot. Having a car opened new opportunities for me. (journey from brooklyn)

My Atomium Club

Sigma Zeta Tau

"I'm Flushed" Bookends

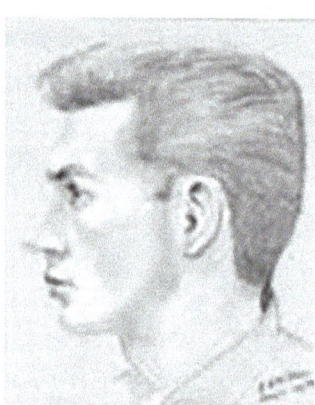
Me, Male Model!

My First Car

CHAPTER 5

COLLEGE GRADUATE…. MARRIED

I did the first quarter of my student teaching at Mount Pocono High School where I taught geometry, physics, and U.S.History. Then I taught chemistry at Stroud Union High School with Mr. Regan as my cooperating teacher. He spent my teaching periods in the faculty room. I didn't learn anything from him. My final post was to East Stroudsburg Junior- Senior High School where Mr. Dimmick was my cooperating teacher. I taught algebra and trigonometry. He took his responsibilities seriously, requiring me to observe him teaching, then he would observe me, and critique my teaching. He had built a podium with five shelves in back. For each of his five classes, he placed each day's lesson plan for each course and the corresponding textbook on the appropriate shelf. What a great idea, I thought, and built one when I started teaching.

I completed all the requirements for my degree in January of 1961. It had taken me only three and a half years. The dean of instruction, had given me special permission to carry an extra load of twenty-one credits during each of my last five semesters. I had received no financial aid. I graduated, married Janet, and assumed my position at Belvidere High School teaching algebra, senior math, and earth science.

Married

Looking back, there were two consequential voids in my life. First, I had never felt loved by anyone. Having never experienced it; I had no understanding of 'being in love'. Second, I had never enjoyed a safe, happy home. I believe that these developmental voids led me to make a bad marital decision, which led to the ultimate failure of our marriage, when I did stumble upon love.

There were times when I felt that Janet was not the right person for me. I should have been more patient, and played the field a bit. Janet was my first girlfriend. She did have a wholesome family. Her parents were very religious. Most

Sundays, several relatives would enjoy a great meal together. Then they would sit in the living room for conversation and a few laughs. I was envious of this family life.

Janet and I had to receive matrimonial instruction at the Stroudsburg Methodist Church. Janet's family had held leadership positions for several generations in this church. Near the end of our instruction, Reverend Stimson said, "David, I will ask you if you accept the Lord Jesus as your savior and redeemer, and you will answer, yes". I told him that I didn't believe that, and would not answer 'yes'. He said that college students often question their faith. I still refused. He asked me to step behind the altar, and we made a deal. He said, "When I ask you the question, simply bow your head and speak softly to yourself, about anything. The congregation will understand your emotion". It worked. (journey from brooklyn)

I invited four of my Russian aunts and uncles to the reception, which was held in the basement of the church. They were shocked. No bar? No whiskey? This was unbelievable. They had never been to a 'dry wedding'. I told them that my wife had never had a drink of alcohol, and that this was the way her family lived. Later, I noticed that two of them went out for a smoke. When they returned, my other uncles went out. They had found a VFW near the church!

Life on the Delaware River

Janet and I found a great house on the Delaware River in Bangor, Pennsylvania, which was only two miles from Belvidere. New Jersey. It was for sale for $9,000. We had no savings, but I convinced the owner, Mr. Otten, to rent it to us for $85 a month, and that I would maintain the property, as if I owned it, still 'controlling my destiny'. There was a PP&L plant a half a mile upriver, which took in water to generate electricity, and released warm water back into the river. This made the river swimmable into October!

I built a dock, and bought a rowboat. I borrowed a neighbor's tractor and cleared the beach to reveal clean sand. Then I plowed the entire property, planted a lawn, and created a garden where I grew melons, cantaloupes, and cucumbers. (see photos)

We had three visits. Commodore Perry came out of nowhere. I had sent him a letter about my college graduation, my marriage, and our address on the river. I think it made him feel good, to see how well I was doing. We had a great visit.

Artie and his wife, Terry, drove out from New York City. We enjoyed swimming off the dock, and later I grilled steaks on the built-in patio grill. (see photo) Then we had another surprise visit. I think that Artie must have told Loretta about our great property. Loretta visited us. We enjoyed swimming and paddling around it my dingy.

[Flash Forward to 1991: I was in my office when Loretta phoned. She told me that an intruder had broken into her home while she was sleeping, threatened her with a knife, and raped her. She assisted the police in their investigation, and had just returned home from the hospital. She asked me what I thought she should do. I told her to take a hot shower, and go to work. Within an hour, I was on an expedited flight to D.C., and then drove to Loretta's home.

When I arrived, the door was locked. A neighbor walked over and told me that Loretta had gone to work. I was waiting outside the law firm where Loretta worked when she walked out. She was surprised to see me. Loretta, always direct and honest, said, "On the phone, you sounded like rape was no big deal, and blew me off". When Loretta phoned me, she intentionally did not ask me to come down; I intentionally did not indicate that I would fly down.

Loretta was divorced and living alone. She had me search the house before she entered (Several years later, a rapist was arrested in NYC. Loretta's rape kit confirmed his identity, as her rapist. Her rapist was convicted). Weeks after my visit, Loretta wrote me several letters. I quote from one: "I am sorry to tell you that I believe Janet to be a very small-minded, seedy, sleazy person who conceals these unsavory characteristics under a cloak of Christianity and motherhood". Her tone and assessment did not surprise me, but the letter did. Janet's name was never mentioned during my visit with Loretta. Moreover, Janet and I had been divorced for about twenty years! I still have the letter]

Years later, Loretta was killed in her sleep when a tree fell on her roof during a storm.

Back at Our River Home

Each day, I would leave work at 3:30 in Belvidere, N.J. and drive to Bethlehem, PA. for my 6:10 class at Lehigh (stopping at home to grab something to eat in the car). Several times, I noticed two men sitting in folding chairs, fishing on our beach. That was okay; until it was not. I noticed that they were leaving beer cans and metal pull tabs in the sand. The next time that I saw them fishing, I went inside, and took out my .38 caliber revolver. I emptied every chamber, making certain the bullets went over their heads. They jumped up and ran, leaving their chairs and poles behind. The following week, I noticed that their chairs and poles disappeared, but the men never returned. Had I more time, I likely would have walked down, and asked the elderly Negroes how the fish were biting, and show them the pail where

I threw my beer cans.

Igor, a Ukrainian Lemko who owned an adjacent lot, had given the gun to me. I had helped him dig an outhouse and build a cabin. What are the odds of two Lemkos living so close together in this relatively remote spot on the Delaware River? Four years later, Igor contacted me, asking to help his son Georgie get into college. I guided him into Syracuse University. Igor repaid me by giving me a motorcycle.

In January of 1961, I was admitted into a master's degree program at the University of Scranton. It was a 130-mile round- trip! My sense was that the professor did not know much about his subject. I talked to my principal, William Stoutenburgh, at Belvidere High School, about the situation. He said that Lehigh University had a great reputation, and was closer to my home. I was admitted to a master's degree program at Lehigh. I also completed eight graduate credits in vocational psychology and counseling under a National Defense Education Act grant at Rutgers University. I taught Janet to shoot the .38 revolver, and moved into a dormitory for eight weeks at Rutgers.

Being newly married and living on the Delaware River, I wondered why I was taking graduate courses at two universities during the summer months. Why was I not spending time at home with my wife? Upon reflection, Janet had difficulty with intimacy. I took her to a gynecologist, Dr. Samet, in Stroudsburg. When Janet returned to the car, she proudly told me "I'm perfectly normal, he suggested that I try having a glass or two of wine before we do it". Janet did not enjoy alcohol. However, she tried the wine, but it did not solve the problem.

At Lehigh University, I took five courses with Professor Edward Scanlan, a brilliant professor with a doctorate from Harvard. I took a course with Professor Milan, and wrote a paper on the 'psychological origins of religion'. When the course was over, I convinced Dr. Milan to engage in an open debate with Dr. Scanlan, who held contrary views on the subject of religion. They debated before a capacity audience. Last year, Professor Milan's daughter sent me his obituary.

Mom Is Out!

I was finishing course work at Rutgers when Aunt Mary called me. She said that Uncle Joe had somehow gotten Mom released from Brooklyn State Hospital, and had taken her to Philadelphia. Uncle Joe had just been released from the Graterford State Penitentiary. He had apparently convinced hospital officials that he owned an apartment building and a dress factory in Philadelphia. He told them his sister could have her own apartment, and work in his factory. Uncle Joe did not own a factory, a home, or even a car.

I drove to the address Aunt Mary had given me. I found Mom living in an SRO (single room occupancy). She was still attractive, but her hair had turned completely white, and the pupils in her eyes danced back and forth constantly. I asked her about that. She said that it did not bother her, and that it was probably from all the electric shock treatments the doctors had administered to the sides of her head over the years. We had a good long talk. She told me that Joe and Sybil, who had a wooden leg, had gone off to work with a traveling circus. I told her that she could come and live with me and Janet. Her response was quick and definitive: "You have to live your own life." She told me that she had a job washing dishes in a restaurant.

The next day, however, we went to a realtor who showed us a small apartment in a private home. As Mom looked around and out the windows, I could tell that she liked it. It was located close to a bus stop, and Mom said that that bus stopped on the corner near the restaurant where she worked. While Mom was at work the next day, I went back to the house and talked with the owner, sharing a little bit about Mom's situation. We worked out an arrangement whereby Mom would pay him a little rent each month, and I would send him a check covering the balance. He agreed to help Mom furnish the apartment. I had my checkbook, signed a blank check, and told him he could fill in an amount for all expenses. We exchanged phone numbers. I was comfortable that Mom would be okay there. I visited her every two weeks. After about six months, the restaurant gave her a job at the counter, waiting on customers. Later, she became a waitress.

Now I Have a Stepfather

Mom surprised me when she got married. I don't know how she and Carl Wilson met. He had been a police officer in North Carolina, but was dismissed for shooting a Black man, without cause. Artie didn't like him from the beginning. I decided to cut him slack, if Mom was happy. Later, however, Carl became abusive to Mom. Artie decided that we should go to Philadelphia where I would hold Carl, and he would smash Carl's kneecaps with a ball-peen hammer. After asking me several times, I finally said, "All right. Get your hammer, and let's go". Artie backed out, which didn't surprise me. He never confronted the Kent Street gang in Brooklyn. He could talk tough, but he never fought.

I drove down by myself. Mom was at work. I started an argument with Carl, and took a baseball bat from my car. My first swing missed him by inches. Carl deflected my second swing, grabbed the bat, and ripped it from my hands. I managed to get into my car, and take off. I did stop at two phone booths, dialed 911, and reported being assaulted by Carl Wilson at 1918 East Willard Street. Mom told me that the neighbors said several police cars came to the house from both directions on their one-way street. Oddly, Carl and I developed a better relationship.

Mom had bought an urban-renewal home for $3,500. When Artie got out of the Navy, we took turns visiting Mom at least once a month. I cannot remember one visit when she did not insist that I "take this money", which was usually between $80 and $150. Artie and I decided to save this money for Mom's future needs. Artie was the custodian of her money. Mom lived to be ninety-four!

[Flash Forward to 2003: A pancreatic specialist at Sloan Kettering Memorial Hospital identified small tumors on my pancreas. I shared this with Artie. One evening, he phoned me and asked, "What happens to Mom's money if one of us dies?" My reply was immediate, "If I die first, you take care of it; if you go first, I'll take over". We agreed. Within minutes, he called back and told me that his wife, Terry, thought that if I died, maybe one of my children should take over my responsibility. I rejected that suggestion. My children lived in distant states, and never had a close relationship with Mom. We left the agreement in place.

A few years later, Artie was diagnosed with liver cancer, and given 60 days. When I saw that he was nearing death, I realized that Artie never told me anything about Mom's money. When I asked him about it, so that I could take over my responsibility, I was shocked by his response. He did not recall any agreement? Thinking the pain medication might have affected his brain, I turned to his wife seated at the foot of the bed, and asked, "Terry, you remember the night that Artie phoned me twice within minutes". Her weak reply was, "No, not really". With anger in my voice, I said "Artie, on your deathbed, you two good Catholics are both lying to me, and you will burn in Hell for eternity". I left.

Days before Artie died, he had a priest hear his confession, and told Terry to give Mom's money to me, as we had agreed. I was shocked to learn that Mom had given us $70,000! Either Artie and I visited Mom more than I remembered, or Artie was a very good investor.]

Our First Plane Ride & Lehigh Master's Degree

Meanwhile, I enjoyed teaching at Belvidere. In my senior math class, one of my students, Dale Ricks, had a two-year-old son. During my free period, Fred Kelly, director of guidance, gave me the opportunity to work with Dale in the guidance office. I discovered that teenagers felt comfortable talking with me. I decided that I would like to become a guidance counselor. (journey from brooklyn)

Around this time, Janet and I went on our first plane ride, which could easily have been our last. While having a cigarette with the shop teacher, Bruce Coullard, we talked about John Glenn's space flight. He was surprised that I had never been in a plane. He invited us to go up in his plane. He lived on a farm in Hope, N.J. There was a trace of snow on the ground. He pulled his plane out of the barn with a rope. Janet and I climbed up and into his plane. She had to sit on my lap behind the pilot's seat because it was a small, skimpy plane. I tapped the sides and was shocked. They were made of canvas. Bruce grabbed the propeller and pushed it down until the engine turned over. He had to do this several times before it started. Each time he cranked it, he jumped up and into pilot's seat. I had a vision of him not getting into the plane in time, and Janet and I flying away without him. But it got much worse, once we were at the proper altitude. I didn't know it then, but Bruce was reckless, and something of a show-off. He showed us too many of his maneuvers!

As a new teacher, I was given unpopular assignments, including the magazine campaign, chairman of the self-study committee, and advisor to the FFA (Future Farmers of America). I took the students to the state agricultural fair. On route, we visited an artificial insemination facility. We watched a worker stimulate the bull to ejaculation. After collecting the semen in tubes, the tubes were labeled, dated, and placed in a freezer. Then they showed us a video of an experimental technique using an artificial vagina. The Warren County Teachers of Agriculture awarded me the degree of Honorary Chapter Farmer!

I did manage to get on the wrong side of school superintendent, Colonel Belet. I had been put in charge of the annual magazine campaign. Two magazine publishers competed for the contract: the company that had the contract the previous year, Shifty Publishing Co., and Curtis Publishing Co. in Philadelphia. After studying the details of their proposals, I decided on Curtis. Mr. Stoutenburgh reminded me that the Colonel wanted to stay with Shifty Publishing, but I recommended Curtis Publishing, and they were awarded the new contract.

Then Principal Stoutenburgh called me into his office, and told me that Superintendent Belet objected to my frequenting a bar on Main Street in Belvidere. It seemed like he was being vindictive. I agreed to stop, but thought the businesses I frequented after work should not have been any of the colonel's concern.

Soon I found a way to strike back. I was the chairman of the self-evaluation committee, prior to the five-year state evaluation of the high school. I worked diligently organizing the committee's responsibilities. One of our recommendations was the need to replace the old uncomfortable wood chairs in the guidance office. During the opening reception for the state evaluators, it was my role to present our committee's report. I called their attention to the recommendation concerning the need for new chairs. I told them that earlier that morning, I noticed new chairs in the guidance office that had not been there the previous afternoon. I stated that I did not know where the chairs came from, or how long they would be there, suggesting that they might want to have that clarified. Later, I was told that Colonel Belet's face flushed when I made those comments. It was a stupid cheap shot.

I met with Mr. Emele, but did not mention my difficulties with Superintendent Belet. I told him that I had received my master's degree from Lehigh University, and was ready to move on. (journey from brooklyn) I decided to look for an out-of-state position. Janet and I applied for positions in the Washingtonville Central School District in New York.

Now I'm a Guidance Counselor

Dr. Donald Van Wagenen, superintendent of schools, interviewed me. Charles Juris, the director of elementary education, interviewed Janet. Charlie became my lifelong friend and gave me invaluable career assistance twenty-five years later! (journey from brooklyn) They offered each of us positions. Janet would teach second grade in the three-room Salisbury Mills school. I would join the guidance department at the high school.

We moved from our Delaware River home to a small cottage on eighteen acres in Salisbury Mills, NY. The owners lived in a large house at the front of the property. The owner gave me permission to park our car in the large barn, to plant a garden, and to use his tractor.

I had formed a personal bond with Dr. Van Wagenen. It began when he and I were discussing a district-wide matter in his office, when his secretary interrupted us, "President Kennedy has been shot". Dr. Van Wagenen closed his office door, walked over to the fireplace, placed his hand on the mantel, and began to sob. Subsequently, in another matter, I intervened when his son, Patrick, was sexually abused by the band director, Burt Hackell, on an overnight band trip. Mr. Hackell was immediately terminated. I was Patrick's guidance counselor.

The following year, the school district advertised to fill a new position, Assistant Superintendent of Schools. I phoned Bill Stoutenburgh, and asked if he might be interested in the position. He told me that he had just completed his doctorate at Temple University, and that the position would be a timely and appropriate promotion. I felt comfortable with Dr. Van Wagenen, and talked to him about Bill. (journey from brooklyn) Dr. William Stoutenburgh was appointed to the position of Assistant Superintendent of Schools in Washingtonville, N.Y.

My employment as guidance counselor proved to be the most satisfying work that I would experience in my life. Several students have stayed in touch with me for years, one student for forty-six years! I met Seth, on my first day of work on August 15, 1963. I was busy organizing my office when the Director of Guidance, Mark Yolles, rushed in. Pointing out my window, he said, "You see that kid…his name is Seth Grodson, he's trouble…broke into Alex's barbershop and stole the cash register. His parents sent him to Israel so that he couldn't be prosecuted. I know he should be your counselee, but I'll take him". I replied that I became a counselor to help troubled kids. I would like to work with him. (journey from brooklyn) He said, "Okay, but you'll be sorry".

Seth stepped into my office, dressed in an army fatigue shirt, which was mostly unbuttoned. I made a benign introductory comment, as he took out a cigarette and tapped it on my desk. My guidance work had officially begun. I said, "Seth, I'm a smoker. This is my first day of work, and I decided to not light up, until I learn what the rules are". He put the cigarette back in the pack. We talked for half an hour, and then he invited me to come over to the lumberyard for lunch, and meet his parents.

The following year, I asked Mr. Grodson if I could work in the lumberyard on Saturdays without pay. (journey from brooklyn) He looked at me and questioned why I would work for no pay. I explained that I just wanted to learn about the lumber business. He liked that, and I got the job. A few years later, Mr. Grodson and I went on a weeklong trip to Virginia, looking for acreage to jointly purchase. I really got involved with my counselees and the people in the community.

Following Seth's graduation, we stayed in touch for the rest of his life. In 1967, we had a great trip to the World's Fair (Expo 67) in Montreal. Then in 1970, Seth knocked on my door in the Bronx. He looked terrible. He had recently returned from Vietnam. He told me that he had a court hearing in a week. I noticed the drug tracks on his arm. He stayed with us until his court date. Judge Robert Samuelson sentenced him to 364 days in the Orange County Jail.

[Flash Forward to 1996: I was retired in Arizona. Seth's father, Julius, phoned me. His wife was suing him for a divorce in Texas. He told me, "David, I need you to meet Seth in Austin. He will give you power-of-attorney papers. Just remember, Alicia doesn't get the house in Round Rock, and I have no assets". Seth and I met with Alicia's lawyers. I knew that Julius had $900K in bearer bonds which were unregistered and untraceable. I told the lawyers that Mr. Grodson informed me that he had no assets. After three days of negotiating, we had an agreement. I signed the house over to Alicia. Her name was not on the deed. Julius never spoke to me again!! In retrospect, I did not represent his interests well. It was entirely inappropriate for me to have injected my personal viewpoint regarding his home, and his wife's needs.]

After Julius died, Seth arrived at my home in Prescott, Arizona. We drove to Las Vegas in his new truck, where Seth, despite my forewarning, lost $15K the first night playing live poker. He thought that he could win it back the next day, but I prevailed. We drove to Costa Mesa, California, and visited two of his buddies from his Vietnam days.

Seth was proud of his son owning a plumbing business, and his daughter a school teacher. Then in 2008, I returned to Manhattan from a visit to Seattle. There was a message from Seth's wife, Joanie. Seth had passed away in a VA hospital. I had phoned him before leaving for Seattle, and he sounded optimistic. Seth was a very good friend, and I was never sorry!

Andy Ratch was another counselee going through some developmental issues. He was a smart kid getting poor grades, and getting into more than his share of trouble. Actually, Seth and Andy both reminded me of my own misused high school years. His father was stationed at Stewart Air Force Base. I'll never forget the first time I met General Ratch. He walked into the Guidance Office accompanied by his military aide. Without saying a word, removed his white gloves, and handed them to the aide. That scene suggested to me what Andy was dealing with at home. The General introduced himself, and peppered me with questions about my background and training, as well as the organization of the Guidance Office. Our meeting was not productive. However, he did take a personal interest in me. He had me flown out to the Air Force Academy in Colorado Springs for a week. It was a propeller plane in which I was served filet mignon.

Later, he was instrumental in having Janet and I admitted to a special program for married couples at Vassar College. He knew that I understood Russian culture and was able to communicate in Russian. The program trained couples to speak fluent Russian. We were told that there were many career opportunities for individuals who spoke Russian. In addition to free tuition, we were paid a weekly stipend. Often, I would enjoy a cigarette with students before class. Oddly, I discovered that none of the married couples had children, **unfortunately, Janet had difficulty with the 32 characters in the Russian alphabet, and we dropped out of the program.** I believe that the program was a Defense Intelligence Agency initiative. It would be interesting to know what careers the successful graduates of the program entered?

Serving as a guidance counselor was a wonderful experience. The Class of 1966 expressed their appreciation in the dedication of their yearbook to me.(see Appendix A)

First Home

Growing Melons 1961

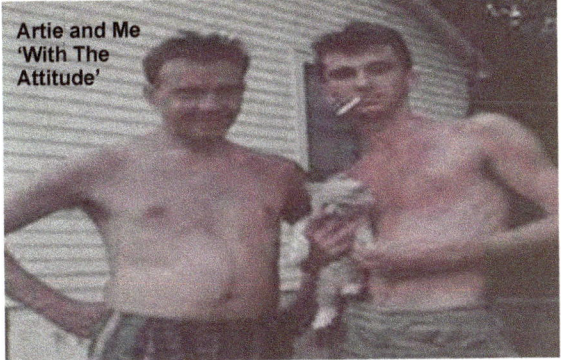
Visiting Mom in Philadelphia

Artie and Me 'With The Attitude'

Mom at 93!

Teaching Senior Math

Rewarding Students - Trip to Manhattan

Plowing My Garden Waiting For Columbia Letter

Chapter 6

DOCTORAL STUDY AT COLUMBIA UNIVERSITY

In 1963, I applied for admission to a doctoral program at Teachers College, Columbia University, the nation's first and largest graduate school of education in the United States. (journey from brooklyn) I had my academic records forwarded to Columbia University from East Stroudsburg State Teachers College, Rutgers University, the University of Scranton, New York University, and Lehigh University, as well as my scores on the Graduate Record Examination and the Miller Analogies Test. My sense was that the interview with Professor Morris had gone well. However, I learned that a follow-up meeting was necessary.

Professor Morris told me that the committee had decided to offer me admission to their MEd program, and if I performed well, I would likely be admitted to the doctoral program. I declined, explaining that I had already completed a master's degree at Lehigh. Professor Morris puffed on his pipe, and asked me to tell him about my personal background. When I finished, he asked one question, "Have you ever been in psychotherapy?" I told him that I had not, and he ended the meeting, telling me that he would take my application back to the committee, and that I would receive the final decision directly from the Office of Doctoral Studies. It sounded as if he was distancing himself from the decision.

I was on the tractor plowing the field behind our house in Salisbury Mills when Janet brought a letter from Columbia out to me. We sat down on the back steps. The letter began with a one- word sentence, 'Congratulations'. That night we went out to dinner to celebrate.

Building a Home

I used to frequent a Black bar on Main Street in Washingtonville, and had gotten to know Larry Peterson. I hired him to cut trees and pull stumps out on an expensive lot that I had purchased in Mountain View Estates. Larry got a mason to pour the basement and build a block foundation. Within six months, Janet and I moved into our own new home.

I had taken out a construction loan to cover the $20,000 cost of the lot and house, and subcontracted out the job. Out back, I built a screened-in patio, which overlooked a pond that I had constructed. I lined the deep pond with heavy plastic and poured concrete over it. I channeled all the rainwater from the roof of the house down into a conduit underground and into the pond. Fish were able to move about beneath the ice in winter. One Sunday afternoon, Professor Morris and his wife, Kate, made a surprise visit to our home. He was always intrigued with my various adventures.

Getting into the StockMarket

I had never spoken with anyone who owned stocks, but I was interested in learning. I would eat my lunch in the car while driving from Washingtonville to Newburgh, and then watch a group of older men looking up at a ticker-tape that moved across the top wall of a room in a stockbroker's office. (journey from brooklyn) They would take notes, and at times go over to a broker's desk. They were not a sociable group, but one of them answered a few of my questions, and told me to "follow the stock market news in the business section of The New York Times".

I took his advice and found the daily fluctuations in stock prices to be interesting. I focused on the daily list of stocks that had reached new highs and new lows for the year the previous day. Trying to figure out why some stocks had hit a low price of the year was extremely difficult back then. I opened an account with $300. It was a 'baptism of fire', as I lost more than I gained, but learned a good deal. I stayed in the stock market for the next fifty years. For the most part, I searched for stocks that had been beaten down to new lows. I was a 'bottom fisherman'.

[Flash Forward to 2015: My new wife thought it would be wise for us to let a financial advisor do our investing. We found a reputable firm in Kingsport,Tn. Between April 17, 2015, and March 1, 2016, our account went down $275,472. I'm back in the markets, and have recovered our losses.]

[Flash Forward to 2009: I took my granddaughter, Sarah, to the financial district in NYC. I had to show her a piece of 'guerrilla art', the famous Wall Street Bull, because he and I both came from Greenpoint, Brooklyn. I learned this when a friend in Israel, Chaim, asked me to go to his storage unit, remove a particular bronze, bring it to Crosby St., ask Arturo to buy it back, and wire him the money. As I came in from the street carrying one of his sculptures, Arturo asked me questions, including where I was from. When I said the Greenpoint section of Brooklyn, he told me that that was where his bull was from. The foundry that cast the Wall Street Bull is in Greenpoint!]

Commuting to Columbia University

It was a 120-mile round trip drive from Washingtonville to Columbia University. I joined a carpool with three guys who were working on doctoral degrees. I sat in the front seat of Charlie Juris's car. Frank Entwistle, school psychologist, and Don Benke, assistant principal, were seated behind us. Once, on the ride back, Charlie asked, "Hey Frank, what did you learn in class tonight?" It was a cruel question, because Frank had been washed out of the doctoral program. Yet, Frank continued to ride with us to Columbia, and sit in the library three nights a week??

Later I learned of others who didn't complete their degree. One unfortunate guy would pace back and forth in the hallway with his head down for hours, mumbling to himself. I asked Professor Morris if he knew anything about him. He told me that he had been a doctoral student in the department that he 'patrols', but had not passed his Oral Exam. He said that guys like that are referred to as having earned an ABD degree (All But Dissertation). I remember thinking, Why the hell doesn't someone offer some assistance to the guy?

Inferential Statistics and Professor Westervelt

Professor Morris was my advisor. At times, he gave advice that I would have preferred not to receive. Once, he told me to register for a course in statistics. I resisted, reminding him that I had already completed a statistics course at Lehigh. "Yes, that's fine, but you need Columbia's statistical inference course". I took it, and received an A+ (Professor Morris said that he had never seen an A+ in this course.) And he was right. The Lehigh course never went beyond chi-square. Columbia's course prepared me to analyze sophisticated empirical research.

Several years later, Professor Morris was a finalist in pursuit of a large contract to evaluate a federal program in Norwalk, CT. I was a member of his team.City officials were interviewing researchers from three universities. During our meeting, a Norwalk administrator asked, "Will you be using tests of statistical inference in your analyses, and if so, what tests will you use?" Professor Morris turned to me, "Dave, will you take this question?" I responded that we would use inferential statistics,only if the data from the pilot study indicate that necessity. And that the statistics used would also depend on that data, and therefore are unknowable at this time. As we drove out of Norwalk, Professor Morris said,"I like the way you handled that, smartass". Columbia was awarded the contract, and it did become necessary to use inferential statistics!

To offset my tuition fees, I became a teaching assistant. Professor Morris suggested that I meet with Professor Esther Westervelt, who was looking for an assistant. Students feared her. She had been a member of the Women's Airforce Service Pilots during World War II where she was selected into a small elite unit which flew night missions. Professor Westervelt mentioned to me that she had a friend in Washingtonville who knew me. Amy Bull Crist was the Orange County Superintendent of Schools. I was her grandson's guidance counselor. That was fine by me, because I knew my counseling skills were exceptional.

Subsequently, I took a required course, which was taught only by Professor Westervelt. Our major assignment was to identify a psychological construct, read everything that had ever been published about it, and then write a report that could not exceed two typewritten pages. I selected 'empathy' and dutifully read everything I could find. I even had to pay someone to translate an article that had been published in a German journal. My first draft was fifty handwritten pages. It was a challenge to reduce it to two typed pages. Professor Westervelt gave me an A on my paper. Her written comment suggested that it was worthy of publication. The article was published in the Spring 1968 issue of the Journal of the New York School Counselor Association.

Later, Professor Westervelt was diagnosed with brain cancer. Professor Morris asked me to drive with him to visit her at Goshen Hospital. It was a difficult visit. She forced a smile and thanked us. She passed away the following month. This was no ordinary woman.

Psychological Consultation Center and Prof. Roger Myers

The following year, I was offered a part-time position as an associate in the renowned Teachers College Psychological Consultation Center. I have no idea how this came about. I enjoyed free tuition which was significant and a small stipend. More important was what I learned working with Roger Myers, Jean Pierre Jordan, Donald Super and Robert L. Thorndike. (journey from brooklyn) To say it was intimidating would be an understatement. We met weekly to discuss an active case. The depth of the analyses, and their perspectives from their specialized areas of expertise and experience were enriching. By far, this was my best learning experience at Columbia University!

I was asked to present a case. At the time, I was counseling a Catholic priest born in Ireland who began preparation for the priesthood at age thirteen.

Father Mac was involved in a relationship with a lady friend, and was torn between that relationship and his 'calling'.

It should be noted, at this time, I had come under the influence of Albert Ellis who had developed a new branch of psychology. His behavioral approach was not embraced at Columbia. Privately, I was taking a course at the Institute for Advanced Study of Rational Emotive Psychotherapy. (journey from brooklyn) Dr. Ellis had supervised my therapy sessions with Father Mac, and had critiqued my sessions.

Father Mac's defenses had been penetrated. The tape I played showed the priest reacting to a strategic intervention. Father Mac stood up, tearing the clerical collar from his neck, throwing it to the floor, and stomping on it. Roger Myers was the first to speak. "Is he suicidal?" "No". "Are you in contact with him now? Tell us about the depth of your relationship with Father Mac". On the way out, Roger whispered, "Nice work, but you took a hell of a risk".

[Flash Forward to 1980: Father Mac had left the priesthood, married, had two children, and held an administrative position in Connecticut working in educational program development.]

Blacks, Puerto Ricans, Chicanos, and Native Americans

The chairman of my department, a gifted professor, Edmund Wyatt Gordon, was the sole Black tenured professor on the Teachers College faculty. (Dr. Gordon just celebrated his 100th birthday.) He and I had developed a good working relationship. Our thinking on social issues was usually aligned. However, I do recall asking for his thoughts regarding the recently released Moynihan Report. In short, he said that Professor Moynihan had been 'intellectually dishonest'. I kept my thoughts private. In fact, I was in complete agreement with Moynihan that the matriarchal structure of the Negro family and the increase in 'welfare dependency' were significantly related to the plight of disadvantaged youth.

At the time, Chairman Gordon was responsible for a project that had been funded by the Ford Foundation and the College Entrance Examination Board. The two individuals conducting the project had abruptly accepted out-of-state positions. Professor Gordon gave me the keys to a storefront on Amsterdam Avenue, and asked me to assess the status of the project. I was shocked at the lack of progress. I reported my findings to Professor Gordon, stating that there was no usable work product. After receiving a second opinion, he asked if I would take over the project. I would have two office workers and $12,000 remaining in the funded grant, plus additional monies diverted from the department's budget. It would be a challenge, but I agreed. (journey from brooklyn) He was sponsoring my doctoral dissertation research.

Having recently read about an upcoming meeting to be held at Antioch College involving individuals who represented Blacks, Puerto Ricans, Chicanos, and Native Americans. I flew to Ohio. The first day, I embarrassed myself by referring to 'American Indians'. Professor Hillfeather stood up, and corrected me. "We are Native Americans". I spoke to him at the end of the session. He introduced me to the leaders of each minority group. One member, Offie Wortham, mentioned that his office had extensive files on many of the college programs for disadvantaged students. That evening I explained to Offie the reason I had invited myself to their meeting, and made a deal with Offie. He wo uld give me ac cess to his files, and I would recognize him and others for their contribution in the report's introduction. (journey from brooklyn)

By the third day, this group became the founding members of the National Association for Minority Education (NAME). Hillfeather agreed to mail me copies of documents on Native Americans that he had accumulated on his campus in Oklahoma. The following week, I drove to Trenton and met with Offie. He did have a treasure trove of documents, journal articles, and reports on each of the minority groups.

Back at Columbia, I prepared a survey which was mailed to every college that had a special program for minority students. My office workers summarized the results, as I compiled a draft project report from all the information that I had acquired. It took me approximately two months to complete the report. Several nights, I slept on a couch in Dr. Gordon's office.

Professor Gordon assembled a group of five individuals to review the draft. We met at the Barbizon Plaza Hotel on Central Park South. The group offered critical observations, but re commended that the revised manuscript be published for widespread circulation. The 575-page report included an introduction acknowledging the contributions of Offie Wortham, Isaura Santiago, David Hillfeather, and Gus Chavez.

Doctoral Residency at Columbia

Janet and I sold our new home in Washingtonville and used the $14,000 profit to finance my residency at Columbia University. We rented an apartment in the Bronx, and moved in with our two children. We were expecting another child in a few months. In 1968, doctoral students were required to sign a statement agreeing that we would not be employed full or part time during our one-year residency. We were expected to be on campus six days a week.

For my doctoral research, I conducted an empirical study analyzing the behaviors of Black college students under various degrees of induced stress. My self-developed data collection instrument was administered to minority students at Essex Community College in Newark, N.J. The instrument was validated as a reliable measuring device. The actual study was conducted using Black students enrolled in the Urban University Program at Rutgers University.

I would be remiss to not acknowledge the assistance provided by Professor Gordon. My research necessitated the administration of a 'sensitive instrument', a Powerlessness Scale, that I had developed based on the Locus of Control research of Professor Julian Rotter at the University of Connecticut. After obtaining the powerlessness scores of each student, I subjected the subjects to various conditions of stress on their campus. As a young white doctoral student (using invasive techniques), I would never have been given access to these students. Professor Gordon had introduced me to the key administrators at Essex College and Rutgers University.

After having collected the raw data, I was given access to the students' academic records as well as disciplinary reports. All data were entered into a computer at Columbia. The results indicated that all four of my hypotheses were rejected. In a state of disbelief, I hired a statistics professor, Dr. Harry Claywar, from City College, to conduct an independent analysis of the data. The results were the same. I was stymied. Even after a couple of months had passed, I had visions of myself pacing the halls mumbling about my rejected hypotheses.

Roger Myers and I had developed a good relationship at the Psychological Consultation Center. One day I met Roger in the cafeteria, and he asked me how my dissertation was going. I was embarrassed, but told him about my results. He urged me to have a sit-down with Chuck (Professor Morris).

I met with Professor Morris, and told him about my results. He asked if he could take my dissertation home, and look over my data. A week later, he called me into his office. He explained that by virtue of 'unintended consequences', my data showed significant results. In short, my results had answered questions that my study had not hypothesized. It made sense, but could I defend it in my oral examination? Puffing on his pipe, he said, "It happens occasionally, but be prepared to explain why you did not ask those two important questions".

As I entered the oral examination, Professor Winthrop Adkins whispered to me, "Dave, just remember, you know more about journey from brooklyn than anyone in the country". While I appreciated his words, I knew that Julian Rotter was the recognized authority on locus of control. (I did know more about powerlessness and poverty than any of my five examiners.) When the examination ended, I was asked to step outside. Finally, the door opened, and I was invited in. The chairman read the results. I had received the highest numerical rating; no editing required!

I received a letter from the Office of Doctoral Studies. It was addressed to Dr. David P. Garrahan. The opening sentence was one word, 'Congratulations', and informed me that my degree would be conferred in May. However, I could begin using my doctoral title immediately. I had triumphed over seemingly insurmountable adversity.

It had taken me nine years (1963-1972). I received no financial aid. My children were now three, four, and five years of age. My dissertation research was published in the national peer-reviewed Journal of College Student Personnel entitled, The Relationship Between Social Activism and Feelings of Powerlessness Among Low Socioeconomic College Students.

Social/Political Activism

I became active in politics in the mid-1960s when Seth's parents introduced me to Phyllis and Sears Hunter. At the time, Sears was the Democratic Party chairman of Orange County. It was he who had introduced me to Robert Kennedy at a fund-raiser in Goshen. (Recently, I Googled Sears Hunter and learned that he had also been involved in President Kennedy's election). I became hooked on politics. (journey from brooklyn) I exchanged a half-dozen letters with Congressman Henry Helstoski, urging him to move forward with the Nixon impeachment initiative in the House of Representatives. Years later, I would develop a personal relationship with Bob Dole. While following the Dole-Kemp campaign for the presidency, I learned that as a result of his WWII injuries, Senator Dole uses a buttonhook to button his shirt every day. I had the perfect buttonhook for the senator. A man whose son had been killed in action had welded the shank of a buttonhook onto a WWII brass cartridge as the handle. Then he had fastened one of his son's medals to the handle, very artistically. Senator Dole expressed his appreciation for the perfect buttonhook in a personal letter. Subsequently, he congratulated me after Haley Barbour nominated me for membership on the Republican National Committee's Advisory Board. (see Appendix)

I have always had a natural inclination to side with the socially disadvantaged. Beginning in 1962, I authored a journal article on the needs of forgotten students at Rutgers University; got involved with the neglected aged population; became active as a Title IX consultant; and supported striking maids employed by Columbia University. The latter involvement could have cost me my doctoral degree because it erupted just weeks before my oral examination. Refusing to cross the striking maids' picket line, I wrote a strongly worded letter to William J. McGill, president of Columbia University. I had dictated the letter to Elinor King, department secretary, and asked her to mail it. She must have mentioned it to Professor Morris because he stepped into my office, and asked me if it was true. I handed him my carbon copy of the letter. Reading it, he became as agitated as I have ever seen him. I paraphrase him: "Do you understand that President McGill has responsibility for all of Columbia University… the Colleges of Journalism…of Business…of Medicine…of Social Work…of Law…of Engineering…Do you think he has time to address your concern about the treatment of maids!" (see Appendix for President McGill's reply).

Dr. Garrahan/Professor Garrahan

Now that I had my doctorate, Professor Morris asked me what my plans were. I had not given it much thought, but was confident that I would have good options. He said, "Professor Gordon wants to keep you at Columbia". He did not offer any specific reason.

The following week, Professor Gordon invited me to lunch. "The college is prepared to offer you a full time, tenure-track, professorial position in the Department of Applied Human Development". This possibility had never entered my mind. "Dave, you have had life experiences that no professor at Columbia has had. You can leverage your disadvantaged life experiences to address critical issues in society. You can create a new graduate course based on your personal history". Expressing my appreciation, I told him that Janet was looking forward to having a home for our children that was outside of the city, but that I would discuss it with her. Janet liked the idea, saying, "We can find a home over in New Jersey". For the most part, I believe that she liked the idea of her husband being a professor at Columbia University.

I gave it a lot of thought. I knew I was not one of them, and had never belonged there—not as a student, and certainly not as a professor. Chairman Gordon had designed numerous programs for disadvantaged youth. He was bringing in disproportionate amounts of money to Columbia through grants from government agencies and major foundations. He had once mentioned to me that as a child in North Carolina, his family had been permitted to shop in white stores one day each week because of his father's prominence in the community as a Black physician. Chairman Gordon had no personal experience with poverty. I understood why he wanted to keep me at Columbia. (journey from brooklyn) With serious reservations, I accepted the appointment to the graduate faculty of Columbia University. Now I was in the major league of academia.

(It is interesting to note that for the two most significant positions in my career, University Professor and District Superintendent of Schools, I did not seek or apply for either position).

Inside My Alma Mater

Chairman Gordon followed up on his commitment, and asked me to design my own graduate course. I developed the syllabus, and taught Educational and Vocational Implications of Ethnic and Social Status Differences, TG4111. (see Appendix)

The following spring, Professor Gordon received a federal grant offering a summer program for directors of inner-city poverty programs from across the country. In April, he asked me to design a program for them. It was to be two hours a day for six weeks, which would be my summer teaching assignment. This was a tall order on short notice, but I knew my role at Columbia (Roger Meyers and I would often play handball on the courts in the basement. One day, as we showered up, he jokingly mentioned that faculty members, at times, referred to me as the 'white nigger' on the faculty!)

I assumed my students would be minority group members. They represented school systems from Detroit, Newark, Los Angeles, Chicago, et al. They certainly knew more than I about programs for the disadvantaged. I knew more about poverty. I used my TG4111 course outline to design their program. Topics included understanding poverty: the thoughts, feelings, and behaviors of the impoverished; spiked with empathy; and empowering the powerless from a locus of control perspective. (journey from brooklyn) The second hour of each day was devoted to best practices and program development, where they learned from each other, and I learned from them. Wednesday nights, they could join me at the Cotton Club in Harlem or the storied West End Bar on Broadway.

At the end of my first semester, I asked Professor Morris for some feedback. His sage advice began with, "Encouraging students to address you as Dave suggests an inappropriate familiarity. The faculty and staff call me Chuck, but I've never been called Chuck by a student. Professor connotes more authority, wisdom, and experience".

Students Dropped by Their Sponsor

During my first year, I sponsored the first of fourteen doctoral dissertations, which were all successfully defended at oral examinations. A few were challenging. Infrequently, a professor discontinues sponsoring a student's dissertation. This presents a huge challenge for the candidate, as well as for the professor who accepts the student at that late stage. In retrospect, I suspect that Professor Morris thought this would be a good way for me 'to cut my teeth'.

One day, Chuck stepped into my office and said, "I can't work with Joyce any longer. It's too frustrating". Joyce was a middle-aged Black woman from Texas. I asked, "Where's Ed on this?" "He couldn't deal with her, and pushed her off on me". I asked Chuck how she got into our doctoral program. He explained that several years ago, Professor Gordon had accepted her on the basis of a telephone interview. I thought, What the hell was he thinking? I'm the one with the reckless reputation. "Dave, if you take her on, you'll have to carry her on your back. If she passes the oral, hopefully, she'll get a Christian education position in Texas, and never mention that her degree had been awarded by Columbia". Given the circumstances under which Joyce had been accepted, Columbia had some responsibility for her progress. I met with Joyce, telling her, "If I take you on, you will have to do everything I tell you to do. There will be no discussion". Within a year, Dr. Joyce went back to Texas. I had stacked her oral exam!

Chuck used the same line when he said, "If you take Sam, you'll have to carry him over the finish line". Sam actually got down on his knees in my office in tears, and pleaded with me. He explained the difficulties he and his family would face if he returned to his country without his doctoral degree. Nigeria had funded his years of study at Columbia. Nigeria was even more violent and corrupt in the 1970s than it is today. We worked well together, and Sam returned to Nigeria with his doctorate. [Flash Forward to 1998: Professor Sam Okon mailed me copies of five articles that he authored, which were published in education journals in Nigeria. He invited me to come to his university as a Visiting Professor. I declined.]

Calvin, a Black doctoral student, completed his dissertation on locus of control under my sponsorship. However, one evening, he and Professor Morris, his advisor, got into a nasty exchange. While I could hear their angry voices, I didn't know what it was about. Cal bolted into my office, and slammed the door shut. "That man is a f*** racist. I'm finished with him, from now on you're my advisor". Standing up, I reached up, placed my hand on his shoulder, and asked him to calm down, and sit down. "Cal, I don't need to know what just happened, but Professor Morris is not a racist". I reminded Cal that he was three months away from his oral exam, and the years of sacrifice by his family. "I am your dissertation sponsor; Professor Morris is your advisor. I will be at your side at the oral". Cal expressed his appreciation in an inscription on his dissertation, in which he thanked me for teaching him 'survival skills'. (see Appendix Z)

Another interesting student was Carl Ransom. He was a navy veteran from Montana. Carl was very intelligent, but in my judgment, 'too rigid' to be an effective counselor. I encouraged him to take a computer course with Professor Taylor. He took it, and got hooked. I recall his wife phoning me to express concern when he began working on a computer in their small dormitory bedroom. I talked with Carl about his interest in programming computers. We visited the college's computer lab. His work was fascinating, and he invited me to give him any problem involving formulating and computerizing solutions.

In short, I asked Carl if he could program a student's college record. Suffice it to note that my wife completed two graduate degrees, our children were 4,5,and 6 years old. There was another student in the 1970's, Vivian Perlis, quoted in the NYT, July 15, 2019 as follows: "I had three children at home, when I asked for some flexibility regarding the requirement to study full time, I was turned down flat by Columbia". Janet did enjoy her anthropology course taught by Margaret Mead!

Sexual Orientation at My Alma Mater in the 1970s

When I was moving into the office across from Chuck's, I asked him whatever happened to Professor Klopf, who had had this office when I was being interviewed for admission in 1963. Chuck said that he had probably sensed that he would not receive tenure because colleagues suspected that he was a homosexual. I was surprised to hear this. Professor Klopf was a well respected professor. Professor Klopf subsequently became the dean of faculty and provost of the Bank Street College of Education in Manhattan.

Several years later, Chuck cautioned me. "You're not helping your Columbia career by working with students like Maurice". Again, I was taken aback by the comment. I had invited Maurice to my home to meet my wife and children. He and I went out for a drink at a bar in River Edge. Sitting at the bar, he said, "Dave, there's something I need to tell you, I'm a homosexual". I almost fell off the barstool. Maurice had been raised on a ranch in the Midwest. "I had to leave. My parents don't know. My brothers don't know". I thanked him for sharing, but cautioned him to be careful on campus.

One weekend he took me out to Fire Island. I knew of the island's reputation. We had a great time darting around the narrow islands in water taxis. Maury knew where all the interesting parties were—lots of drugs, alcohol, and interesting dancing. He was a good student, and I liked him. As I prepared to leave Columbia and join the faculty at the University Maryland, I took great care in finding a colleague who would take Maurice through his oral exam. Professor Joseph Grannis agreed to sponsor Maurice. [Flash Forward to 1996: I received a phone call at my home in Arizona from Elinor King, department secretary, asking me whether I would consider opening an incomplete grade that I had given a student. I said, "Sure", and specified the conditions. Then I took the opportunity to ask about Maurice. "He didn't make it", she said. When I left Columbia, he was on a clear path to his doctorate. I do not know if Maurice's sexual orientation was a factor that caused him to not complete his dissertation.] Maurice still lives in Manhattan.

Subsequently, I began serving as an oral examiner at college- wide exams. I gained a reputation for my skill in analyzing research design and the statistical methods employed. Apparently, I was too severe in my examination of one candidate. The morning following that oral examination, Chuck stepped into my office to tell me that Professor Max Wise was very upset because I had blindsided him with my critique of his student during the oral exam. The candidate had not established the validity or reliability of his instrument. I told the oral examiners that because of that critical defect, it made no sense to discuss his results. The oral ended. Of course, I was right. Professor Wise had not read his candidate's research very carefully, if at all. Moreover, he should have made a more studied judgment of my posture as an oral examiner, since I had previously fired a shot across his bow. In that case, the student he was sponsoring had used an analysis of covariance model, which I knew to be an inappropriate statistic for his study. It should have been clear that I was not one to turn a blind eye, regardless of the sponsor's status.

Too Much Partying

Over the next five years, I made presentations at professional conferences in Detroit, Miami, San Diego, Boston, Atlantic City, and Chicago. The one in Chicago was unforgettable. I always tried to have my presentations scheduled for the beginning of a convention, so that I could then relax, and enjoy my surroundings. In this case, I did make my presentation the first afternoon. But then I took the subway to an antique store where I knew the owner had very unique 'glass buttonhooks'. I found the place and bought all three, but then I got off at the wrong subway station. As soon as I exited the station, I realized that it was not the right neighborhood. There was a bar at the top of the exit. I went in for a drink, and directions. It was a Black bar. I took a seat, and put money on the bar. The bartender saw me, but ignored me. I said to the guy on my right, "What do I have to do to get a drink?" "Go somewhere else", was his response.

The guy on my left, however, called the bartender down, and I was served. I also got directions to the Palmer Hotel where I knew there was a party. Carole White, a

Black doctoral student, had invited me. I found it and got involved, forgetting that we were interviewing an applicant for a psychology department position the following morning. When I woke up on the floor and looked around, there were several Black folks asleep in the room. I asked the woman closest to me, "What time is it?" She said, "My watch is in the top drawer". When I opened the drawer, the watch was on the wrist of a B lack artificial arm. The face of the watch was not visible, so I had to turn the arm over. I was late for the 10 a.m. interview. I got out of the room quickly, and ran to the Teachers College's suite in their hotel. I paused at the door, gathering my wits and composing myself.

Chairman Myers opened the door and looked at me with his small, dark, piercing eyes. "The interview is over. The candidate left ten minutes ago", he said. I nodded my head without uttering a word, walked inside and peered out a window at Lake Michigan, as thoughts raced through my mind. Then my colleagues exploded with laughter. Yes, I was late. However, the applicant had missed his flight in St. Louis. We interviewed him at 4 pm.

Teachers College, under contract with the Agency for International Development had been involved in educational development in Afghanistan between 1954 and 1978, publishing school textbooks, and 'other activities'. It was widely believed that the Afghan Project also served as a cover for national intelligence personnel. We also knew it as an assignment for faculty who had drinking problems or sexual relationship issues. During my tenure, four of my colleagues accepted assignments in Afghanistan. They either accepted the assignment or resigned their position.

Roger once cautioned me, "Keep it up, and you'll wake up in Afghanistan". He mentioned my relationship with Allegra Bennett, a Black assistant in Chairman Gordon's office. Then he reminded me of a recent episode. My colleagues and I had dinner at the storied West End Bar, but then stayed too long.

While crossing Broadway, Professor Andy Anderson stumbled into a parked car, cutting his forehead.

Professor Jordan and Chuck grabbed him under his shoulders, and walked him back onto campus.

At the precise moment we entered the door to Horace Mann Hall, President Cremin was exiting. He stared at us in disbelief. Jack Foley, Tom Niland and I tried to hide behind Chuck, Andy, and Jean. President Cremin said, "Charles, I'll speak with you in my office in the morning". The following morning, Chuck stepped into my office. "How did it go?" I asked. "I've got to get Andy into a program or he's going to Afghanistan". The following year, Andy was posted to the Afghan Project. I talked with him when he returned. It was a tough place to live, if one was a drinker. Teachers College reported Andy's death in a newsletter and quoted his wife: He died from liver cancer.

Riding with and for Chairman Gordon

Professor Gordon would often ask me to join him when he was making a presentation in a distant location. On one such trip, we drove to Providence, Rhode Island. It was a long ride with lots of time and questions. "Did you read Professor Cottons's book?" he asked. "Yeah, Counseling and the Self Concept", I replied. "Give me a synopsis", he asked. "You'd have to look at the bibliography". "Why do you say that, Dave?" My response was, "I don't recall much original thinking". Gordon continued to press on, asking, "Any thoughts on his commitment to disadvantaged folks?" "Skin thin" was my curt reply. Chairman Gordon valued my perceptions and directness. In 1974, I was appointed Deputy Chairman of the Department of Applied Human Development.

On my last trip, Chairman Gordon asked me to go 'in his place' to a memorial service in Great Barrington, Massachusetts, for Shirley Graham Du Bois (wife of W.E.B. Du Bois). I got into the car with three Black men whom I had never met, and we drove to Great Barrington. It was a long uncomfortable ride. Professor Gordon did not tell them anything about me, and I had no interest in revealing my background to strangers. I was one of three white people at the Mahaiwe Cemetery. At one point, I found myself looking up at two linemen at the top of a telephone pole doing work on the wires. The guy next to me leaned over and said, "If you don't have an FBI file, you'll have one next week".

The ride back to NYC was more comfortable. The men were certain that the guys atop the pole had a camera on us. We talked about that. I revealed that I was one of the founding members of NAME. Interestingly, two of the guys knew about the organization. By this point, they must have been curious about me.... Du Bois memorial, NAME, young white guy? I considered sharing that I was Columbia's 'White nigger'. However, I chose to not disclose. (journey from brooklyn) While I knew nothing about Shirley Graham Du Bois, I had read a great deal about her husband, W. E. B. Du Bois, and joined in the conversation with my car mates. He had been the first Black person to receive a doctorate from Harvard University. He was a scholar, writer, professor, historian, and a member of the Communist party.

I served Chairman Gordon well on that trip, and yes, I assume that I have an FBI file. Several folks at the Palmer Hotel struck me as being more than serious Black activists. The NAME group certainly would have been fertile ground for surveillance.

Chuck's Gone

One day, Chuck stepped into my office, and closed the door behind him. He had never done that before. He sat down and said, "Dave, I think I'm dying". Just like that, one sentence. I asked him about his symptoms. Over the previous month or so, I had noticed that he appeared weak and preoccupied. He had not seen a doctor, nor had he told his wife, Kate. Why me, I thought?

I urged him to phone Columbia Presbyterian Hospital, schedule a diagnostic evaluation, and talk to Kate that night. I visited him in the hospital. He died within weeks. His body was not processing protein? Following his funeral, Kate shared with me that I was the only person, outside of the family, who he had allowed to visit him in the hospital.

Chuck had interviewed me for admission to Columbia in 1963. He had driven up with Kate to see the home that I built in Washingtonville; had resolved my dissertation data problem; had mentored me as a neophyte professor; and hadn't seemed to mind the roaches on the couch where he and my mother had been sitting (she with a can of beer in her hand and cigarette in her mouth). I wonder if he ever told Roger about that visit. Chuck had ribbed me when I became 'his boss' as deputy chairman of the Department. He had steered me clear of trouble more than once. He was a good guy, a regular guy. I missed him. It would never be the same for me at Columbia!

Making Some Extra Money and Having Lots of Fun

With my Columbia doctorate, I had decided to monetize the degree. During my tenure at Columbia, I had been appointed to the adjunct faculty of the Union Graduate School (UGS) at Antioch College. No one at Columbia was aware of my dual role—not even Chuck. Unlike Columbia, I had some colorful students in the UGS doctoral program.

My first student was Sy Weissman. I had interviewed him for admission, but concluded he did not meet Columbia's standards. However, because he had twenty years of significant administrative achievement, I suggested UGS as a viable option. I sponsored his dissertation, and held him to Columbia's standards. He received his PhD. (A decade later, Brooklyn District Attorney, Liz Holtzman, indicted him, charging multiple counts of grand larceny. When I saw Sy's photo in the N.Y.T., I phoned his lovely wife, Betty, and asked if I should go to his Forsyth Street office and 'clean out his files'. She had no idea what I was alluding to.)

Other individuals who I mentored through their Ph.D. degrees included Steve Aiello, the youngest President of the NYC Board of Education. He later served in the White House as special assistant on ethnic and urban affairs to President Jimmy Carter.

Dr. Harvey Garner became New York City Schools Chancellor. Harvey and Steve were major league players. Luigi Miele was not. The colorful Luigi Miele came to the US from Italy as a teenager. My sense was that he was 'connected'. Whenever he visited my home in Demarest, he would give each of my young children a $10 or $20 dollar bill. Once, he foolishly walked into my office at Columbia and handed me two sets of round-trip tickets to Fort Lauderdale. He said, "Go and take one of your friends. Relax and enjoy staying at my motel on the beach". Two of Luigi's sisters operated the motel. It was January; Professor Foley and I did indeed enjoy ourselves.

When the time came for Luigi's oral defense, I knew his committee members: Colin Greer of Brooklyn College, and a retired Harvard professor whose name now escapes me. He passed the oral, and to celebrate, he had booked the entire basement at Mama Leone's in Manhattan. In my opening remarks, I mentioned that I was intrigued with how Luigi had gotten the 'bit part' of cleaning up tables at the wedding party in the original Godfather. Luigi did become a successful entrepreneur. He established the Fordham Beauty School and the International School of Foreign Languages. He is probably best known for his Italian Hour radio program, broadcast from White Plains.

My next venture started at Columbia. Chuck had stepped into my office holding a letter in his hand. "Professor, I could use a favor. The National Association of Trade and Technical Schools (NATTS), requests that a member of the faculty serve on an accreditation committee to evaluate the Delehanty Institute on Union Square", he said. (journey from brooklyn)

The two-day visit was boring, but I did like Delehanty's president, Tom Souran, and his Ukrainian Lemko secretary, Vera. My sense was that the NATTS group was biased against Delehanty, and I refused to be a signatory to the final report. They reluctantly appended my minority statement. When Tom received the results and cover letter stating that NATTS's accreditation was not being restored, he invited me to dinner. I learned that the Delehanty Institute dates back to 1913. By 1942 it was the largest war-work training school in the country.

Delehanty was bringing in a lot of money. Somehow, Tom had acquired copies of the NYPD's promotion exams. By 1975, 90% of uniformed police and 80% of its firemen were Delehanty graduates! Any cop who was eligible for promotion to sergeant or captain was required to pass an exam. Delehanty was the place to go for the three-night preparation. This was a 'cash operation'. Several nights, I noticed Vera shoving the money into a canvas bag. Tom was a good friend of Sandy

Garelik who was the first Jewish Chief Inspector in the NYPD, and later became President of the New York City Council.

I told Tom that it was not likely that they would be re- accredited by NATTS. He put me on a $600 a month retainer, and sponsored my associate membership at the NY Athletic Club. I had John Lansing, Admissions Director, clean up their recruitment procedures. I convinced Tom that there was no future for the radio-repair program. Their other programs were solid. Then, I initiated the Delehanty Digest, and wrote articles for each quarterly issue.

As a member of the evaluation team, I knew that Delehanty's 'finances' were a major NATT's concern. After consulting with a law professor at Columbia, I had Tom set off the police/fire-training component as a separate entity, which would not be subject to accreditation purview. Then I hired a bookkeeper, Mr. Szymanski, to maintain the financial records. Sam was an interesting gentleman. I asked him about the numbers tattooed on his arm. He explained that he had been a prisoner in a German concentration camp. He assured me that Delehanty's financial records would satisfy both state and accrediting auditors. Sam stayed with Delehanty for years.

On a parallel track, I found an accrediting agency in Illinois that agreed to conduct an evaluation. At the end of their first day, Mr. Souran walked us over to a Greek restaurant on Union Square (Tom is Greek). The visitors really enjoyed their dinners. Delehanty received accreditation by the National Association of Accredited Business Schools. As an expression of his appreciation, Tom gave me one of the coveted offices with a curved window overlooking Union Square Park! I stayed on retainer for several years. In October of 2019, my son, Mark, and I visited 853 Broadway. The curved glass windows were removed. Fortunately, I had photographed the windows in 2018! (see photos)

Subsequently, I received a phone call from John Lansing. He was now the Director of the Eastern School for Physicians Aides at 85 Fifth Ave, a few blocks north of the Delehanty Institute. His wife, Loretta, was a personal friend of Emilio Benenati, owner of Nell Joy Industries, a worldwide aeronautical components company. Emilo had bought the school, and made John the director. The school had lost their NYS charter. John told me that Mr. Benenati wanted to meet privately with me. I drove out to Copiague, Long Island, and had dinner with Emilio. In a nutshell, he made it clear that he wanted to keep the school, and keep John in NYC.

There are two conditions that can be fatal for a private school: loss of accreditation and loss of a state charter. Loss of accreditation can be addressed more easily because these organizations need schools to monitor. State agencies have no such need. Emilio put me on an $800 a month retainer. On Teachers College,

Columbia letterhead I wrote to Dr. Kenneth Briggs,

N.Y.S. Education Department's head of vocational education in Albany requesting an appointment. We met and reviewed the list of deficiencies. I asked Dr. Briggs what his department's preferred remediation was for each deficiency.

Within weeks, I sat down with John Lansing and developed a plan. The dental technology program had too many issues. We closed it and transferred students to another tech school in Manhattan. The staff for the medical assistant programs was very weak, and would be difficult to deal with. The fact that the school had no library would be relatively easy to bring into compliance. I found a retired hematologist, Dr. Mangrum, who had authored a book on hematology, and hired him. Then I found two Russian medical doctors, who were studying for the examination to be licensed to practice medicine in New York.

They were excellent. It was a stretch, but New York State issued me a license to teach a medical assistant course. (I never taught the course, but it was impressive to have four doctors in the school's catalog). The school had an unoccupied office which became a library. With Eastern's credit card, I went on a buying spree at the nearby Strand Bookstore. On weekends, I had the walls painted, replaced the ceiling light fixtures, carpeted the floors, and hung a few framed career related posters.

I wrote a carefully crafted letter to Dr. Briggs. Enclosed with the letter was a single-page delineation of the work we had completed at the school. In the letter, I asked for his department's guidance as to our next steps. He sent two staff members down to reevaluate the school. The Eastern School for Physicians Aides received their state charter!

Then Mr. Benenati, surprisingly, bought the entire second floor in the adjoining building (87 Fifth Avenue). This was a huge financial investment. He obtained a New York City permit and removed the two walls between the buildings. The Eastern School for Physicians Aides expanded, and became the Eastern Technical School (ETS). I developed new programs in graphic design, licensed practical nursing, and business office management. I also initiated the ETS Bulletin, and gave the commencement address in 1980. I maintained a retainer relationship with ETS until 1983.

Mark Likes Pasta

Mark Likes Pythons

Playtime

Delehanty Institute Office Curved Glass Window

Eastern Technical School 85-87 - 5th Ave

Both come from Greenpoint, Brooklyn

Chapter 7

FROM COLUMBIA UNIVERSITY TO FROSTBURG STATE UNIVERSITY

Back at Columbia, Roger and I had a serious talk. I asked him candidly how I was being perceived at the college. "You're very good at what you do, but you're a hustler. You spend a lot of time on your private consulting. You're never on campus on Fridays. Everyone likes you, but there's talk". He also reminded me about my relationship with Ms. Bennett. He did note that my NVI(national visibility index) score was appropriately high.

Roger was spot on. Typically, professors in the graduate schools of Columbia University taught five courses during the academic year. I taught three courses in the Fall and two in the Spring, which equated to ten clock hours of instructional time each week. I was conscientious with regard to my non-instructional responsibilities. I always monitored my advisee's progress, and never refused an opportunity to serve as an oral examiner. Many professors made regular time to write books and journal articles. For example, Professor Donald Super would close his office door in the morning and devote two hours to his publications. That was not for me.

Through my work at Delehanty and Eastern, I developed a reputation within the tight knit technical schools in Brooklyn, Manhattan, and the Bronx, and had begun addressing their issues. I also continued to evaluate and reorganize programs and departments in public school systems. I had founded the Institute for Human Resource Development offering consulting services, seminars, and grant writing assistance. My Columbia department's gerontology program was well aligned with the Office of Aging in Washington. Privately, I offered seminars for nursing home administrators in the tri-state area.(see resume in Appendix)

Title IX had been enacted in 1972. Most institutions and employers were not prepared to deal with the requirements. I had completed a federal training program, and was certified as a Title IX consultant.(journey from brooklyn) I learned how the U.S.Department of Education's Office of Civil Rights (OCR) enforced the law. OCR also conducted "proactive investigations" (Compliance Reviews). Consulting opportunities abounded. I could easily have done this work full time through my Institute, and would have likely doubled my income.

However, another variable in my career decision-making was related to my relationship with a doctoral student, Eileen Goldstein, who I had never taught. (journey from brooklyn) Her dissertation necessitated the use of sophisticated inferential statistics. Her sponsor, Professor Foley, had no relevant expertise. Her co-sponsor, Professor David Wilder, understood canonical regression analysis, but misused his position attempting to curry favor. Cleverly, Eileen had discretely tape recorded one such encounter at a restaurant on the Saw Mill River Parkway. I became involved, critiquing her research design and statistics. We had a good working relationship which became personal.

Holding my seventeen-year marriage together was my priority. My good friends among the faculty, Chuck, Tom, Jack and Andy were gone. Chairman Gordon was comfortable with my consulting, and encouraged me to stay at Columbia. However, I was not comfortable with 'shortchanging' Columbia. It made sense to reset and relocate.

After pondering the matter, I asked Roger and Ed to write letters of recommendation. Gordon wrote, "His colleagues at the college and in the profession readily turn to him for leadership". Roger wrote, "It is my strong hope that he remains at TC, Columbia, and were he to do so, I would readily accept him as a member of the department of psychology faculty".(see Appendix) I applied for a position at Frostburg State College, University of Maryland, and resigned from my position at Columbia. At Frostburg, I was appointed associate professor of psychology, and the director of the graduate school's programs in counseling psychology, guidance and counseling, and social work.

I sold my home in New Jersey, and bought a house in LaVale, Maryland that I thought Janet and our children would enjoy. Back in Demarest, Janet began packing. During my first week at Frostburg, I left my office to find a restaurant in town to have lunch. As I exited the building, I could hardly believe my eyes. There on the front steps was Eileen. She had flown into Keyser, West Virginia, rented a car, and drove to Frostburg. Life gets complicated!

Fast Start

It was something of a culture shock when I moved from Columbia University to Frostburg State College. Getting off to a fast start, I rewrote the fieldwork placement guides. I strengthened the curriculum by adding three new courses, and dropping others.

My faculty had their offices scattered about the campus. One professor had his office in a teacher-training facility, which included an elementary school. He brought his dog to his office every day. The faculty members each had reasons for having their offices where they were. They were comfortable. I explained the importance of having departmental offices in one location, both for the convenience of students, as well as for the development of 'program identity'. My words fell on deaf ears.

Quick Finish

Finally, with the approval of Vice President Kenneth Jablon, all course changes and all office reassignments were implemented by the end of the first semester. One professor, Otto Spielbichler, appreciated what I was trying to accomplish. I took Otto to the American Personnel and Guidance Association's convention in Washington, DC where we made two presentations. The rest of the faculty remained uncooperative, attempting to undermine my initiatives. In retrospect, it is clear that I moved too quickly, and in a heavy-handed manner. I resigned at the end of the second semester.

After seventeen years, Janet and I decided to get a divorce. There was no love in our marriage. The relationship was wrong from the onset. Something important was missing, and I was becoming more uncomfortable with my infidelity. Janet and I began by going to a stationery store where we bought a divorce kit. Together, we prepared a divorce agreement. It included both alimony and child support. When we were both satisfied with our agreement, we hired an attorney, Al Tanney, to execute it. He advised against representing both of us, but finally agreed. Janet was granted custody of our children. Mr. Tanney charged us $2,100 (the legal fees for my most recent divorce were $45,000!). I assisted Janet in buying a home in New York, where she lived until her retirement. Mr. Tanney called our attention to the fact that we had made no provision for the college education of our children. Janet wrote a codicil which stated that we would share all college expenses in proportion to our respective incomes at the time our children went off to college. Her handwritten page was appended to the divorce agreement.

When our children went off to Alfred University, American University, and Salem College, Janet refused to honor the provision that she had written. To avoid litigation, I assumed total financial responsibility. It is interesting to note that when our daughter, Susan, was eighteen years old, and then when Dean was seventeen, they each asked me if they could live with me and my wife, Eileen. We welcomed them into our home in Pearl River, New York. Susan and Mark have maintained lifelong relationships with Eileen.

I'm a Guidance Counselor, Again!

I phoned Dr. Weissman and told him I was coming back to N.Y.C., and needed a position with flexible hours to cover my expenses until I found work. (journey from brooklyn) Sy came through giving me an office at 65 Court Street, which was around the corner from the infamous '110 Livingston Street' where Dr. Garner and Dr. Aiello were positioned with the Board of Education. I moved into an apartment on Park Ave with, Roberta Feller, Eileen's good friend.

As I pondered my next career move, I considered my options: a university position, private consulting, or a role within the NYC school system? (journey from brooklyn) However, Dr. Goldstein pointed out the advantage of receiving a state pension. That reminded me of how I had enjoyed counseling high school students. I decided to seek a high school counseling position.

Pascack Valley High School in NJ hired me as a guidance counselor. I was back to where I had been in 1963—working with teenage students. The other counselors tried to convince me to stop meeting the school buses in the morning to greet my counselees. "Is that what you learned at Columbia?" But it was a good use of time, because I could touch base with a dozen of my kids each morning. I was doing a great job, and enjoying my work. It was very satisfying for four years.

I'm a Director of Guidance

Teaneck High School advertised for a Director of Guidance. A decade earlier, Teaneck had hired me as a consultant to conduct a district-wide assessment of their guidance and pupil personnel services. Now I would have the opportunity to see how my recommendations had been implemented. (journey from brooklyn)

I was appointed Director of Guidance. During my first week, I posted a schedule of visiting college admissions counselors who would be available to meet with students the following month. The next day the principal, Jim Delaney, walked into my office, and threw the crumbled-up notices on my desk. "Don't ever put anything up in this building without my initials". His tone was revealing. I made a quick assessment. At the end of the day, I spoke with Dr. Green, school psychologist, who had been a doctoral student at Columbia. She confirmed my assessment. Given my work style, and his psychological transparency, it was clear that I would not be free to properly administer the department. I decided to leave. (journey from brooklyn)

I'm a Director of Pupil Personnel Services

In a February, 1983 issue of The New York Times, I spotted a listing for Director of Pupil Personnel Services in the Northern Highlands Regional High School District in Allendale, N.J. I applied. There were three inside candidates. I knew that if the competition was open and fair, the position would be mine. It was fair. I was granted an early release from my Teaneck contract.

In March, I took over as director with the responsibilities for guidance, school psychology, social work, and special services. This was a wonderful opportunity in an affluent community.

I decided to also carry a caseload of fifty students as my counselees—doing what I really enjoyed. One of my counselees was Beth, daughter of Bernard Arnold, president of the board of education in Allendale, N.J., a very 'waspy' town. As we approached the end of my first successful year, Mr. Arnold spoke privately with me. He shared that he was not satisfied with the performance of our district superintendent, Gerald Hopkins. He delineated his numerous concerns. "I want you in his position", he said. I explained that it was not possible because I was not qualified. Moreover, I could not be certified by the state because I did not have the requisite six years of administrative experience in New Jersey. Nor had I taken the required courses for state certification, which included school administration, school finance, and education law. Bernie was persistent!

Not Qualified and Not Certifiable

One day, I was attending a meeting in the County Education Office. During a break, I found the smokers' room. A lone woman, Ms. Poschaski, was inside enjoying a cigarette. She mentioned that she handled certification issues for the county. I thought to myself that if I applied for state certification as a school superintendent, I would obviously be rejected, and this would put the nutty idea out of Mr. Arnold's head. (journey from brooklyn) So, I asked the woman about the procedure for applying for superintendent certification, mentioning that I lacked almost all the state requirements. She asked about my professional background.

Then she suggested I assemble my credentials, and mail them to a specific individual in the Office of Academic Credentials in Trenton. "Do not request a waiver of requirements or any course substitutions", she said. I mailed my credentials. Within a month I received my certificate as a 'school administrator' destiny control/ Not. This is crazy and not possible, I thought. I asked my friend Dr.

Goldstein to contact the state, and ask what positions a person would be eligible to hold with certification as a 'school administrator'. The shocking answer was, "Any and all school district administrative positions in New Jersey"!

As I reflect back on this encounter in the smokers' room, my guess is that Ms. Poschaski assumed that I wanted to be certified as a superintendent. I did not want or expect that outcome. In fact, I wanted to be rejected. I knew nothing about running a school district! She probably told her 'contact' in Trenton to see what he or she could do to help me out. There is simply no other reasonable explanation to explain the outcome. Just think, a cigarette with a stranger, a brief casual conversation, and my life was changed.

I enjoyed challenges, but this would be beyond the pale. Mr. Gerald Hopkins had been the founding superintendent of the district. He had led the school district since its inception in 1963. Bernie Arnold was unique. When he learned that the state had certified me. He went into action, and offered Mr. Hopkins a generous retirement award in cash and not taxable. Mr. Hopkins took early retirement. The Board asked me to interview for the position. They offered the superintendency to me. I accepted. It was a very controversial appointment.(see Appendix)

CHAPTER 8

SUPERINTENDED GARRAHAN

The Northern Highlands Regional High School District (NHRHS) serves the residents of Allendale and Upper Saddle River, New Jersey. It is an affluent community populated by corporate executives, lawyers, and bankers—most of whom commute into Manhattan. The town attracts a disproportionate number of major league athletes, including Lawrence Taylor, Lou Piniella, Jim Burt, and Bill Parcells. The infamous former FBI Director, James Comey, graduated from NHRHS.

I expected the position to be a challenge. Soon, I would learn that the challenges exceeded my expectations. The Board president, Arnold, made his objective clear to me when he said, "I want you to clean house, and make NHRHS one of the top ten high schools in the United States". I thought, does he know that there are more than 25,000 public high schools in the country? Bernie had set the bar high. Expectations in the community were also elevated. I was well aware of my own unqualified experience for the role, and made no pretense to the contrary.

Upon entering the superintendent's office, I pulled open every file drawer. Yikes! Someone had removed everything. Dropping in new hanging folders, I labeled three: State Education Department, County Education Office, and Teachers Union. This was the extent of my knowledge about being a superintendent. Typically, a new superintendent will work together with the departing superintendent for a period of time. Obviously, this was not to be.

It is important to note that in the history of the district, the board had never developed a job description for this leadership position. More interesting is the fact that during my ten years as superintendent, I never had a contract. This was at my request. When the board offered me the position, realizing my limitations, I told them I did not want to tie them into a contract. I explained that if at any time a majority of the board became dissatisfied with my performance, they should just tell me, and I would resign.

[Flash Forward to 1995: As I prepared to retire, I went to Trenton to meet with a retirement counselor. The young woman was shocked to learn that I had never had a contract. I thought, What's the big deal? I just want to make sure that I will receive a pension. She conferred with a superior, who came in to confirm that I had never had a contract. Her supervisor said this is a 'first', as she never heard of a superintendent working without a contract. She asked if I had any vacation days left. I told her that in my ten years, I had never taken a vacation. To my surprise, she told me that the district would be required by law to reimburse me for each of my unused vacation days, at my current salary. It came to $120,000! My board was also shocked. I couldn't do this to them, but who throws that kind of money away? I did, and accepted $60,000 as full payment.]

Start with a Controversy

My appointment was very controversial. A prominent outspoken community leader threatened a lawsuit on the basis that no female or minority applicants had been granted an interview. Others charged that there had been no search conducted at all. Bernie Arnold wanted me to run the school district. In silence, I agreed with the disgruntled taxpayers. However, state officials ruled that my appointment was legal.(Appendix)

A few weeks into my new position, I received a phone call from a reporter for The Scranton Times. He had written an article entitled, Trouble Maker Student Now Heads School District, and wanted to verify several points before publishing the story. I have no idea how the newspaper learned about me. Within a week, the article was in the hands of Allandale and Upper Saddle River residents, many of whom had opposed my appointment. Most people understood that teenagers could do dopey things and get into trouble. I sure did!(see Appendix)

First Week: Two Very Important Lunches

My first week in the position, I took the chief of police, Frank Parenti, and the editor of the Town Journal, Mary Service, to separate lunch meetings at a Spanish restaurant in town. (journey from brooklyn) It seemed like a good idea; actually it proved to be a great idea! Chief Parenti was most appreciative, mentioning that superintendent, Hopkins, had not spoken to him in his entire 36 years as chief of police in Allendale!

I established good rapport with these two important community people. For example, a few years later, kids were pulling the fire alarm once a week, and we had to evacuate the school as firemen searched the building. I met with the chief, and explained that when the alarm went off, my security guy would reset it, and that it would take a few weeks until I can have cameras installed to monitor every alarm box. (Later I would learn that it was not only students who were setting off the alarms!) Frank had a private conversation with the fire chief. (see Appendix) Later, the vice principal, Vinni Herold, was arrested on a DUI with an underage female in his car. Mary Service called to give me a 'heads up'.

The story would be in the next issue of the Town Journal. I asked her to reconsider. She said, "I saw the video of him slobbering all over the police station". I pleaded that this story would be damaging to our school and community. With great reluctance, she killed the story. Vice Principal Herold rode a bicycle to work for a year!

My friend and car mate from Washingtonville, Charlie Juris(sans doctorate), was now the superintendent in Ridgefield Park, N.J. He phoned to give me a heads-up that my business administrator, John Kowalsky, might become a problem. Charlie said, "He's very headstrong and doesn't accept guidance from his superiors. He's also a drinker".

One day, I asked Kowalsky to join me for a drink at the Ramada Inn. Sitting at the bar, I mentioned that I asked questions because I needed to learn about tax rates, contracts, vendors, filing state reports, etc. He replied that he ran the Business Office, and implied that he didn't want me nosing around. I said, "You will follow my orders". John reminded me that I didn't know anything about school business. Sensing that he was challenging my authority, I said that he would follow my directives, or else. "Or else what?" he responded. Looking at him, I said, "You f*** with me, and I'll bring someone(Bulldog) from out of state to blow your legs off ". Staring at me, he said, "You're crazy", got off the stool, and left. (At the time I didn't know that Kowalsky was a Ukrainian Lemko). We worked very well together for years until he retired.

My Initiatives Are Not Well-Received

It should be noted at the outset, that my leadership style has always been very autocratic. I never had any use for committees or 'group think', and I was never concerned about being 'politically correct'. I met with the department supervisors, asking them to review their course offerings, and directing them to submit copies of all teacher evaluations to me. Their reaction was that they never forwarded teacher evaluations to Mr. Hopkins, and thought that it was unnecessary. I saw it as a way for me to learn about the teachers, as well as the quality of their departmental supervision.

I initiated the practice of meeting with all of the school district's administrators after school every Friday in my conference room. If we had a public event during the week, I would lead a critique of the event. Their posture was 'if it ain't broke, don't fix it'. However, I believed that there was always room for improvement. The meetings were not productive.

Later, I dropped Latin from the curricula, and added a computer education course. The Teachers Union objected. The Latin teacher retired, and Latin was phased out. I engaged a consultant to design a computer education course in concert with our business and mathematics teachers. The Board approved my recommendation that the new course become a required course for graduation.

Another initiative involved having some of our top students take courses at a local college. A senior executive at Ingersoll Rand Corporation lived in Upper Saddle River. With funding from IR, and support from the president of Ramapo College in nearby Mahwah, we established the Rand Scholars Program, whereby selected students received college credit for courses during their senior year. The administrators and supervisors resisted the program because of the logistics and paperwork involved in transporting the students to the college, adjusting their schedules, and calculating their grade point averages. In time, I sensed that the staff's attitude toward me was rooted in something beyond my leadership style.

An Interrelated Faculty and Administration

I talked to Bernie. He gave me a historical perspective. Our current board attorney, Al Caputo, had been the town's attorney back in 1962. He had advised the mayor and council to hire a consultant to lay the groundwork for the new school district. The consultant that they hired was Charles Mintzer, the father of Jack Mintzer, my principal. (Bernie told me that Mr. Mintzer had been the only other candidate that the board had interviewed for my position.) The consultant recommended that Gerald Hopkins be appointed as the district's first superintendent. And Mr. Hopkins hired Jack Mintzer as his principal! Hopkins and Mintzer had been employed by the district since the very first day, and had hired the entire staff that I inherited!

Most of the staff were interrelated by personal, family, or social relationships. Many believed that I had been involved in the forced retirement of Mr. Hopkins. Now, I understood why cooperating with me was not a priority. This was going to be more challenging than I had anticipated. Not only was I not prepared to administer a school district, but there was a bias against me from the outset. I reflected…I had resigned from my Frostburg position after ten months, and had resigned from Teaneck after seven months. This board of education had resisted community pressure, and had confidence in hiring me. I saw no choice, but 'to soldier on', and earn acceptance and respect.

Drug Use, School Security, and Rudner

My sense was that many students were involved with drugs. Accordingly, I designed a drug-use survey, and sought the cooperation of all students. After perusing the results of the survey, I was convinced that the students had responded honestly. Analyzing the data, it was clear that we had a drug problem. I told the board that we needed a school security program. It was a hard sell in 1985, in an affluent school district. On a split vote, the board agreed to hire two security officers.

I met with Chief Parenti. He suggested that I hire a retired police officer who knew the community. While that was good advice, I decided on Chris Rudner, a 22-year-old graduate of NHRHS. He had walked into my office without an appointment. I knew nothing about him. After an hour, I was convinced that he knew many of the students using drugs, as well as where the drugs were coming from. I also liked his style and self confidence. Realizing that this would be a 'hard sell' with the board, I met with Bernie, and told him that I needed his help in getting the board to approve Rudner. Bernie knew the young man. It seemed that everyone knew Rudner. Bernie said it would be better if I followed Chief Parenti's suggestion, but I persisted. (journey from brooklyn) I recall Bernie telling me, "David, if this doesn't work out, it's going to be bad for you". But he pushed the appointment.

The board reluctantly passed the resolution appointing Chris Rudner, Director of School Security. He turned out to be the best hire I ever made!

After the security program had been in place for three months, Rudner issued the first school security report. He delineated the number and nature of incidents that had resulted in the arrest of several individuals from outside of our two towns. These individuals had been arrested for selling drugs to our students on the school's campus. Rudner also had about a dozen additional security cameras installed.

We continued the drug survey for three years. One finding related to the factors that might influence a student to 'not get involved with drugs'. Surprisingly, it was the students' concern with their health, more specifically, with their personal appearance. One day, I phoned Bernie to tell him the Waldwick Fitness Center was upgrading their equipment, and auctioning off their existing equipment. I had asked Carl Mortensen, supervisor of health and physical education, to take a look at the equipment, and get some idea of what we might bid. Bernie told me to get the money from Kowalsky. We had the winning bid. (Absent the Board's prior approval, this purchase was illegal.) We tore down a wall between two classrooms near the gym and installed the fitness machines, and mirrored the walls. The kids loved it. Subsequently, I authored The Application of a Systems Approach to Substance Use Prevention: Linking Interventions to the Infrastructure. The article was published in the Journal of Alcohol and Drug Education. The longitudinal data from the study was incorporated into a meta analysis in the Netherlands.

Banning Foreign Travel

My unilateral ban on all student group trips to foreign countries caused an uproar. Terrorists had begun hijacking commercial airplanes. We had sister schools in France and Spain. The board backed me, but several teachers, on their own, began planning student trips.(teachers take these trips at no personal cost!) Some parents wrote letters to the editor of the Town Journal stating that my order was unconstitutional.(see Appendix)

Implementing an Eight-Period Day

I convinced the Board that an additional forty minutes of instruction would enable graduates to be better prepared for college. The Board agreed, and voted unanimously to add an eighth period to the school day. I anticipated resistance from most teachers and the Teachers Union, as well as an outcry from students. Some teachers began wearing sweatshirts with 'No 8- Period Day' emblazoned on the front of them. While I had publicly supported an increase in teachers' salaries to compensate them for the additional class and the lengthened school day, apparently, it had not been generous enough. When teachers protested by refusing to enter the building, I was forced to close the school for a day. (see Appendix)

The union bought a full-page ad in the Town Journal censoring me with a vote of 'No Confidence'. (see Appendix). Students presented a petition to the board, signed by half the student body. Even parents objected to the increased demands on students, putting them under additional stress. Finally, the union and the board negotiated a salary increase. We lengthened the school day, and teachers received a hefty increase. Obviously, I had underestimated the ruthlessness of the union.

NHRHS Seeks National Recognition

Every superintendent in the United States receives information concerning the Federal Secondary School Recognition Program. I was reminded of Bernie's desire to have NRHRS as one of the top ten high schools in the country. At a meeting of the Bergen County superintendents, I learned that New Jersey had never participated in this national competition.

Superintendents perceived the competition as an unwise time-consuming distraction, and all school districts in N.J. agreed to not participate. Obviously, this was self-serving. Teachers and school administrators do not want more paperwork.

I discussed the competition with the board. They asked why excellent high schools in Princeton and Ridgewood had never entered the competition. No high school in N.J. had ever entered. I told the board that we would probably learn what other good schools across the country were doing, and that it would require some extra time. As soon as word got out, superintendents began calling me with words of discouragement. Their school boards were pushing them to enter the competition. They were not happy; I couldn't care less. (journey from brooklyn)

We received notice from Washington, D.C. that we had qualified for an on-site evaluation. The evaluation team would consist of educators from states other than New Jersey. I was responsible for getting groups of teachers, supervisors, parents, and students ready to meet in evening sessions with the visitors. During the day, visitors would observe classroom instruction, gather test scores and school records, and conduct private one-on-one interviews within the building. I was directed to reserve a block of rooms at a motel that had conference/meeting rooms.

I had Rudner take the school van to meet our visitors at the airport in Newark. Rudner was very late returning from the airport. Finally, the van arrived. Rudner, being Rudner, had decided to give our visitors a tour of Manhattan, and to treat them to dinner in Little Italy! He whispered to me that they had enjoyed three bottles of Italian wine. "I loosened them up for you, Doc", he said. Rudner had a great sense of humor.

National Recognition: We Did It!

I received a letter from William Bennett, the US Secretary of Education, informing us that NHRHS had been selected as one of the exemplary high schools in the country. I responded by doing something I rarely did. I went on the school's public address system. I announced, "We are one of the top high schools in the country. There is no higher recognition". I could hear the cheering throughout the building.

The newspapers covered the story extensively. They wrote that property values would go up (The New York Times), and our graduates would be even more attractive to the elite colleges. It was a coveted recognition. We were invited to the Capitol and greeted by Secretary William Bennett. President Reagan praised our achievement in a Rose Garden ceremony. I met with Senator Bill Bradley. Back in Allendale and Upper Saddle River our residents were jubilant (see Appendix).

Declining Enrollment and Increasing Taxes

During these first few years, I had taken note of our school's declining student population, as well as the high property taxes. Some residents were paying more than $15,000 a year in school taxes. I was concerned that this would eventually have a negative impact on the quality of education. It was obvious to me that regionalization was the answer. I had published several articles on the subject in leading state journals. The solution would be to merge our district with school districts in one or two of our contiguous towns. (journey from brooklyn)

One K–12 school district would yield significant economies of scale: one superintendent of schools, one special education department, one school bus vendor, etc. Under one regionalized school district, each town would spend less money, and their children would receive a vastly superior K–12 education. Most importantly, we could streamline K–12 curricula. This is particularly important in foreign language and mathematics. Property taxes would be reduced. At the time, there were seventy-seven separate school districts in Bergen County!!

In Allendale, the Hillside Elementary School and NHRHS were both located on Hillside Avenue - six blocks apart! I ran the high school district; Dr. Tom Morton was the K-8 superintendent. Clearly, the two districts should be merged. Likewise, in our Upper Saddle River feeder school district, they had their administration, textbooks, vendors, etc. I simply tried to achieve the highly desirable and logical merging of three districts into one district, so that residents would see a significant reduction in their school taxes, and all students would receive a better education. To me, this was the definition of a 'no-brainer'.

Rumors began to circulate in the communities. One that irritated me the most was that I was promoting regionalization in anticipation of becoming the superintendent of a new enlarged K-12 school district. I took that possibility off the table by telling the Town Journal that I would resign from my tenured position, and that I would not apply for the superintendent position of a merged school district, nor accept the position were it to be offered to me. Everyone had to know that I truly believed in the obvious merits of regionalization.

The bottom line was that none of the local school boards thought regionalization was a good idea. Approximately twenty board members would lose their elected positions. A regionalized district would simply have one board of education. I realized that the idea of regionalization was a losing battle. This is an example of the government's waste of tax dollars. It was the most frustrating experience in my entire ten years.

For Sale: A High Quality Education

I convinced my Board that in view of our recent national recognition, we could probably attract tuition-paying students from outside our district. We agreed on a tuition rate of $12,000, and that parents would be responsible for their children's transportation. I placed ads in newspapers from Tuxedo Park, NY to Demarest, NJ. I actually went door-to-door in affluent communities, ringing doorbells, and handing out an impressive twenty-three page booklet describing our education and student activities programs. We attracted thirty-two tuition students the first year, which brought in about $350,000. It was good, but not good enough. Moreover, it took considerable time and effort for me to find these families. Also, many tuition students came with 'baggage'.

Let's Make a Deal

I thought about the possibility of convincing an entire town to bus their students to NHRHS. I spoke privately with our Board president, Dr. Nick Rotunda. He gave me the go-ahead to see what I could do. There was only one logical town, Ho-Ho-Kus. Like NHRHS, this was a very affluent town. For twenty years, they had been sending their entire class of eighth-grade graduates to Midland Park High School. Midland Park was essentially a blue-collar town. My perception was that their tax base was reflected in the quality of their high school.

I phoned the president of the Ho-Ho-Kus Board of Education. Without telling her the reason for my call, I invited her to lunch in Waldwick where the likelihood of our being recognized was small. I told her that our meeting and conversation must be kept private. Then I broached the sensitive subject. NHRHS's recent national recognition had been in all the local newspapers. I noticed a sparkle in her eyes. She thought this idea had great potential. We agreed to discreetly seek feedback from key individuals in our respective towns.

A few weeks later, we met again. She said that every person with whom she spoke was surprised to learn of this possibility. She thought that Ho-Ho-Kus would jump at the opportunity. We then agreed to meet in executive session, closed to the public, with our respective Boards.

I designed a tuition model, which was both clever and inviting. It was an offer they could hardly refuse. (journey from brooklyn) The tuition during the first year would be $8,000. At the time, they were paying $9,200 to Midland Park. In four years, there would be a slight increase. Subsequently, tuition would become significantly higher, but would be subject to negotiation.

Her Board was enthusiastic. My Board struggled with the implications. I told them that this was entirely my idea, and that we needed to do it. Board attorneys were engaged to work on the issues involved. Midland Park's superintendent, Auggi Presco, phoned me to say that he had heard a rumor, and that surely, it wasn't true. I said, "It's true". Auggi had a hot temper. I was determined. Ho-Ho-Kus was in the middle of a three-year contract with Midland Park.

The merger became a huge story in the press. Mr. Presco was quoted as stating that the tuition rates proposed by Northern Highlands were out of whack. Of course, he was right. Our cost per pupil was $12,000 per year. The proposal I had offered Ho-Ho-Kus was $8,000 for the first year. I was playing dirty pool. Our Board and the Ho-Ho-Kus board finally voted to consummate the proposal. Midland Park filed a lawsuit against Ho-Ho-Kus. They cited 'breach of contract', and violation of the N.J. constitution. [Flash Forward to 1996: I received a call at my home in Arizona from Jamie Plosia. "Dave, the New Jersey Supreme Court just ruled in favor of Ho-Ho-Kus and dismissed Midland Park's lawsuit with prejudice".

It was nice of Jamie to remember who had initiated the merger which put the NHRHS district in a very favorable financial position. As of January 2021, Ho-Ho-Kus and the Northern Highlands Regional High School district are still contractually bound in what clearly has been a win-win relationship.] It was the best initiative that I had ever taken.

No Martin Luther King Day at Northern Highlands

Criticism of my position regarding Martin Luther King Day had been bothersome. There were very few colored people in Greenpoint, Brooklyn in the 1940's. When I was about five years old, Mom was holding my hand as we walked up Java Street to the Avenue. Walking in front of us was a woman with two children, who crossed to the other side of the street. A colored man and woman were now walking in our direction.

We passed each other on the sidewalk. No words were spoken. But then my mother said, "Colored people are just like us, they just have a different color skin". That was an important lesson for me. I had never seen a colored person. Mom could have crossed the street, or she could have pulled me closer, and squeezed my hand. Had she done so, I likely would have internalized a negative message about colored people.

To be clear, my bona fides are well documented: In Support of Recruiting Negroes (1970), Founding Member of the National Association for Minority Education(1971), Friends of the East Harlem Block Schools(1971), Study of Compensatory Programs for Disadvantaged Youth(1972), Feelings of Powerlessness and the Success of Socially Disadvantaged Students(1972), Relationship Between Social Activism and Feelings of Powerlessness Among Low Socioeconomic College Students(1974), Documenting Racism in American Social History(1993), Military Tradition: African Americans in Military Service(1994). In 1977, I went in place of an African American to represent him participating in the Memorial Service for Shirley Du Bois at the Mahaiwe Cemetery in Great Barrington, Massachusetts.

Rev. Martin Luther King was a complex man. He was a courageous leader in the Civil Rights Movement. His sacrifices and achievements are well known. Less well known is the dark side of MLK's life. In the June 5, 2019 issue of the New York Times, the author cites the research of David J. Garrow, a Pulitzer prize-winning biographer of the Rev. Martin Luther King. Dr. Garrow is a man of the Left, a self-described, democratic socialist. He has always been an admirer of King. Yet, Garrow methodically documents the unsavory aspects of Rev. King. Attorney General, Robert F. Kennedy authorized the FBI to wiretap MLK's home and office phones. I believe that the FBI went beyond RFK's authorization when they began placing recording devices in MLK's motel rooms, and sending the taped recordings to Coretta.

The June 18, 2019 issue of the Wall Street Journal included: A Reckoning With Martin Luther King. Quoting, "Mr. Garrow has reported, in sometimes pornographic detail, on King's assignations with some of the more than 40 women, single and married, with whom he is said to have had affairs.(intentionally omitted by author). Those close to King, including journalists covering the civil-rights movement, were aware of his womanizing and drinking--though they did not know the extent (intentionally omitted) parishioners. Mr. Garrow's information, however, appears to be solid. He is a painstaking, widely respected historian. The material in his article is not based on hearsay, but on newly released, vetted summaries of the FBI's audiotapes, which are themselves sealed until 2027. Any remaining doubts should be settled seven years from now, when the public will hear King's familiar voice on the tapes. Mr. Garrow predicts that the shock will be considerable".

My primary reason for not closing school had little to do with MLK. Rather, it was the loss of instructional time. Yes, every minute is important. Often lost in the voluminous Coleman Report, mandated by the Civil Rights Act of 1964, was the significant correlation between the number of instructional minutes and student achievement. It is the reason that I fought so hard to add an 8th period to the school day. It was also the reason that I denied almost every student and teacher request for what I considered to be non-essential activities, often suggesting that the activity be sponsored by school clubs or community groups.

My Board asked me to close the school for Martin Luther King Day. I refused. We had five or six Black students. If they decided to celebrate MLK Day, it would be understandable. If we closed the school, however, most students would not observe the holiday. Some would hang out at the Paramus Mall, and flirt with trouble. Board members were concerned that we would be perceived as racist. Board president, Dr. Rotunda, reminded the board members, "Dave has never seemed to care what people thought of him". I explained to the board, that as the school's educational leader, it was incumbent upon me to ensure that our students receive the very best education possible, and that every minute/hour of instruction was important... more important than being 'politically correct'. In ten years, I never closed the school on MLK day. I peered through my window at the protesters blocking traffic. They were doing what they believed was right; so was I.(see Appendix)

A week before the holiday, Lawrence Taylor (LT of NFL fame) had come into my office. He was a resident taxpayer. I explained my thinking to him about the importance of instructional time. I also mentioned that MLK had plagiarized his doctoral dissertation. Two independent commissions concluded that large portions of his doctoral dissertation had been taken from other individual's work, which he represented as his work-product. Boston University should not have awarded him a doctoral degree. LT understood my point. Two years later, LT and I were on opposing basketball teams for a fund-raiser. When I was about to take a shot, he came up behind me, and pulled my knee socks down. The crowd roared. It was a fun move by LT.(see photo)

Anonymous Allegations

Meanwhile, the problem with the inbred staff continued to fester. It is difficult to imagine the extent to which some educators will go to protect the status quo. Someone shot a bullet through the window of my home. Then Mary Service phoned me with a heads-up. The Town Journal had received a copy of an anonymous document that detailed my alleged misdeeds. I stopped at the Town Journal, and picked up a copy. It was bad, and it had been mailed to each member of the board of education, as well as to the mayor, and members of the town council. The five-page document included allegations of misuse of public funds, inappropriate sexual conduct, drunken episodes, and my high salary.

The new president of the Board, James Ryan, called for an emergency meeting. The Board would meet with me in an executive session. It was two hours of discomfort for all of us. I addressed each of the allegations, separating fact from fiction. For example, one afternoon, my secretary called Rudner into my office. I was asleep with my head on the desk. Chris Rudner, Vinni Herold, and Buddy Ajalat managed to carry me, in my chair, out the back to Rudner's truck.

I woke up in the bed of the truck, and looked out from under the tarp. I thought, Oh no, Main Street, Allendale. They took me home.

I did enjoy a couple of Manhattans with dinner at the Seven Seas on the district's credit card. I did this when there was a late board meeting. These were often eleven-hour days for me. Some were much longer. One unforgettable Board meeting found me sitting at the conference table with one last member, William Leonard, who insisted on going into extreme detail on everything. The wall clock indicated that it was 2:15 a.m. Mr. Leonard fell asleep at the table. I had heard that he suffered from narcolepsy, and I phoned his wife. She advised me to make sure that he didn't fall and hit his head. Then she explained that he could hear, and understand everything that was being said. She told me to continue the meeting, as if he was awake! I dutifully went on with the meeting, asking him questions, and explaining my position on issues. I even explained why I did not hire his daughter to teach social studies! When Bill awakened, he thanked me for calling his wife, and answered the questions that I had asked while he was sleeping!

As to my sexual misbehavior, I described a business dinner that Kowalsky and I had with the district's bus vendor, Mike Ely, at a Spanish restaurant in Allendale. I happened to notice a lone woman at the bar who appeared to be sobbing. Placing my hand on her shoulder, I asked her something. She said that it was her fortieth birthday, and that she was alone. I invited her to join us at our table, and we cheered her up. Believing that she ought not drive, I took her home, and met her wheelchair-bound mother. Later I learned that the bar boy, a NHRHS graduate, recognized me, and mentioned it to a teacher.

I waited outside the conference room as the Board deliberated. When I was called back into the session, there was recognition of what I had accomplished, and confidence that I would continue to achieve at a high level. They told me that my personal life was just that, and to keep it personal. This was a courageous Board!

Draining the Swamp

Now the gloves are off. I'm from Brooklyn. I convinced the Board to pass a resolution promoting the longtime Board attorney, Al Caputo, to the sole role of handling special education litigation. He resigned. I phoned Charlie (my carpool pal from the 1960's), and asked him who was the best school board attorney in New Jersey. Without hesitation, he said Jamie Plosia. The Board appointed Mr. Plosia as our attorney.

I made another call to Charlie. I said that I had some personnel/ organizational problems. I needed a reputable consultant who was 'open-minded'. "Take a look at Savitt Associates out on Long Island", he replied. I convinced the Board that we needed to hire an independent consultant to analyze our organizational structure. After sending out requests for proposals, I recommended Savitt Associates. (journey from brooklyn) The Board awarded the contract to Savitt Associates.

Dr. Savitt's team did a thorough study. When he presented his findings and recommendations to the Board, all hell broke loose in the school and community. Principal Mintzer was quoted in the Town Journal as saying, "The consultant's work was a legalized hit-and-run job" (see Appendix). The Savitt report made a strong case for the restructuring of the administration, and a redeployment of staff. Now, it was incumbent upon the Board (which had paid the consultant with taxpayers' money) to follow through with the effort, and approve actions to implement the Savitt report recommendations.

A public meeting was held, which drew a large agitated crowd including reporters for the Bergen Record and the Town Journal. Mary Service put it succinctly when she wrote:

"The Town Journal has talked to the participants in the dispute — what emerges is a deep division between the Superintendent, Dr. Garrahan, and the Highland's staff, and a resistance to change by the staff. At the same time, harassment has been directed at Dr. Garrahan's family, with anonymous letters saying that he won't have a job next year.

Yet, Principal Mintzer and two teachers stated that Highlands is a family". She went on to write, "The superintendent supports the consultant's recommendations. The Principal, Mintzer, does not, nor do the teachers, nor does the president of the union, nor does the executive committee...

Dr. Garrahan would not speculate about the reasons for the staff ' s strenuous opposition to implementing the report ... nor could he suggest who orchestrated the campaign of harassment ... an anonymous five-page handout has circulated among Allendale residents the past few weeks, critical of Dr. Garrahan's salary, and questioning why Principal Mintzer is being reassigned". After the dust settled, a dozen staff members resigned from their positions. (see Appendix)

I Was Forced to Resign

Next, I went after remaining members of the old guard. Most accepted a monetary payout which is illegal in New Jersey. A few others dug in their heels. The last holdout was tough. After placing a voice activated recorder on the bookshelf in my office, I invited Robert Manzo to come in to discuss his thoughts regarding retirement. When I thought I had collected enough of our conversation, I suggested we think it over, and talk the following day.

When Mr. Manzo returned the next day, I played the tape. He became enraged, jumped up, and ran from my office, yelling that I had taped him. He returned to my office the following day, and asked for the tape. I reminded Bob that he had left our previous meeting without listening to most of the tape, and that he had made comments that he would never want anyone to hear. I handed Manzo a 'suggested' letter of resignation, and told him that the tape would be destroyed after the Board accepted his resignation. Two weeks later, the Board accepted Mr. Manzo's resignation.

Subsequently, Manzo contacted Mary Service at the Town Journal, telling her that I had taped him illegally, and forced him to sign a prepared letter of resignation. At the next meeting of the Board, Manzo had packed the meeting with his supporters. He accused me of illegally taping a private conversation. Under these circumstances, he asked the Board to rescind their prior action. The Board held its ground, and voted unanimously to not rescind his resignation. I cleaned house, Bernie. The swamp has been drained! (see Appendix).

National Recognition: A Drug-Free School

For years, I had collected reliable data relating to our students' drug use, in particular, the reasons why most students avoided drugs. I requested literature from the US Department of Education, Office of Safe and Drug-Free Schools. As I completed the application, I described specific changes that we made in the school which were designed to discourage students from 'experimenting' with drugs. I was reasonably certain that no other high school in the country had approached student substance abuse from the perspective of 'substance use prevention' as NHRHS had. We entered the national competition. I did have some concern. One can never predict how residents, many of whom disliked me, will respond to outside inquisitors. The evaluators had private meetings with students, teachers, nurse, social worker, school physician, and residents. They spoke with parents, police officials, and others who might have information regarding student drug use.

In June 1993, I received a letter from U.S. Secretary of Education, Richard Riley, stating that NHRHS had been designated a Drug-Free School. NHRHS was one of only 20 high schools nationwide to receive this recognition! We were invited to Washington, DC where our host was to be Senator Ted Kennedy. However, Senator Orrin Hatch greeted us, and explained to me that his friend, Ted, had an important date. We were recognized in a Rose Garden event. (see Appendix) Our community was again cited in The New York Times.

A Battle Royale

Following the resignation of Principal Mintzer, I was tasked with finding a replacement. Our employment listing in the New York Times attracted fifty highly qualified candidates from across the country. I interviewed the top five contenders, and recommended Dr. Geoffery Gordon . He had impressive credentials, letters of recommendation, and an engaging personality. The Board interviewed Dr. Gordon, and appreciated why I had recommended him. As I had been appointed to be the school district's second superintendent, Dr. Gordon was appointed as the high school's second principal. As newspaper reports show, he was popular with students, staff, and parents. In fact, I cannot recall one person who did not like him. He was a great choice … or maybe not?

About three months into his position, I met with Dr. Gordon to discuss a program. During our conversation, one of his responses did not ring true to me. I thought Molly Wellen, Director of Pupil Personnel Services, might be able to confirm what he had told me. After telling her what was on my mind, she stated emphatically, "That's simply not true". A red flag went up. I confronted Dr. Gordon. His face flushed red, and he said, "Well, what I actually meant was". I interrupted, "No, Geoff, you lied to me". I dropped the matter and moved on, but didn't forget. A few months later, Rhoda Ferat, social worker, spoke privately with me. She raised a concern about something she had heard from a student. "It's probably nothing, but I thought you should know". I gave a lot of thought to the implications of what Mrs.Ferat had told me.

One night, I gained access to Dr. Gordon's office. The keys to his file cabinets were in his top desk drawer. I found personal correspondence and other material that had nothing to do with Northern Highlands. I hid a voice activated micro- cassette recorder in his office. While I could only hear his voice in the conversations, I heard enough.

There were no grounds to remove Dr. Gordon based on the execution of his administrative duties. I could not remove him on the basis of my psychosocial assessment. While I did have the audio tapes, I never released them. Yet I did what I believed was the right thing to do. I had learned that New Jersey education law provides a superintendent with the inherent power to block any personnel appointment. Everyone in the school and community assumed that Dr. Gordon's contract would be renewed. As soon as word got out that Dr. Gordon's reappointment had been removed from the Board's agenda, wild rumors began circulating in the community.

Subsequently, we met in my office. Dr. Gordon came with a high-profile NJ labor attorney. I had shared the information that I had gathered with Mr. Plosia. His attorney asked to listen to the audio tapes; I refused.

When it became clear that my position was immovable, the two lawyers caucused in my conference room. When they returned, they said that the nature of the subject called for a 'gag order' which they had prepared. Dr. Gordon and I signed it. Shock, disbelief, anger, accusations, and bizarre rumors followed. The newspapers covered the known facts. It was very frustrating for members of the community. The only people who could answer their questions were held silent by the gag order. Dr. Gordon was paid $1 for his resignation! And I agreed to give him a letter of recommendation. I did; it was a statement in which he was damned by faint praise! I thought, Why would an innocent man resign? (When Chris Rudner read my book, From Brooklyn to Kingsport, he phoned to tell me that Dr. Gordon had subsequently been abruptly terminated from two administrative positions in other school districts.) I Googled Dr. Geoffery Gordon. In a 2/5/18 news story, I read: "Tenafly school chief quits suddenly after six months in his position". And a 3/26/19 newspaper article stated, "District officials would not comment on why Dr. Geoffery Gordon was placed on administrative leave". Apparently my concerns, however unpopular, were well founded! (see Appendix)

Senator Bill Bradley

Senator Orrin Hatch

NJ. Gov. Jon Corzine

DC Award Ceremony

Allendale Police Dept

LT Pulls Socks Down

Speech in Traverse City, Michigan 1990

Chapter 9

END OF MY JOURNEY

One night, a police officer came to my home in Pearl River. He asked to step inside. "Can we sit down? Your son Dean is dead. He took his own life". My life was changed forever.

Dean was twenty -six. He had a college degree in environmental science. He was employed in the Florida Everglades doing work he enjoyed. His girlfriend had left him, returning to her ex-boyfriend.

I had dealt with many problems over the years, but I was not able to deal with this loss. I began drinking too much, and taking various drugs. One night, I was at home sitting on the couch drinking vodka. Eileen was in the bedroom. Three men in white uniforms came in the front door(which had been left unlocked), walked toward the couch stating they were here to help me. When one went behind me, I stood up, and resisted. They wrapped straps around me and carried me into an ambulance. I saw one preparing a hypodermic needle. I yelled, "I don't want to be injected with anything!" He stuck the needle into my body.

Superintendent in the Psychiatric Ward

I woke up in the Frawley Psychiatric Unit of Good Samaritan Hospital in Suffern, NY. Receiving no response to my voice, I managed to get the gurney to the door. It was 3 a.m. on the wall clock. A nurse rolled me back into the room. A psychiatrist began asking me questions. I told him that I would not make any more disturbances, if I could phone my lawyer. He had a nurse bring me a phone. (journey from brooklyn) I called Rudner. "Hello, Mr. Rudner. I know lawyers don't appreciate calls at this time of the day, but I'm strapped to a gurney across from the nurse's station in the Frawley Unit at Good Sam.

I need to get out of here as soon as possible". I thanked the doctor and nurse. I knew that Rudner had decoded my message. Rudner is sharp. Within an hour, he walked into my room, and showed me the razor. "Let's go". As we rushed out of the room, the nurse yelled, "You can't leave. It's snowing out. You don't have shoes". We broke into a run for Rudner's truck.

The next day, Rudner got me an ill-fitting suit of clothes. In the evening, we went to my home. My wife refused to open the door. She would not put my wallet, medicine, and keys out the pet door! We left, but planned a forced- entry for the following morning when my wife would be at work. The next morning, Rudner and I waited across the road, out of sight in a neighbor's driveway. Eileen never left the house because there was too much snow. Our mission was aborted.

I remembered a woman who worked at the County Courthouse in New City. Years earlier, I had helped her with some personal problem. She put me at the top of the Judge's calendar. (journey from brooklyn) The judge asked me to stand in the crowded courtroom. I answered his questions. He asked me which car I wanted. I replied that the Cadillac was Eileen's, and that I would take the Volkswagen. The judge issued a court order to enter and live in my home. I told the judge that the home was owned by my wife. He explained that under NY law, this was my home.

I arrived at 93 Pascack Road with a locksmith and a lawyer with a video camera. My wife came to the door, and denied me entry. The lawyer read the judge's order, to no avail. I told Kevin to drill through the lock.

My wife was screaming on the phone, "They're drilling the lock". She unlocked the door. My lawyer handed her the court order. She packed a suitcase and left.

Meanwhile, the Board had met with me in an executive session. They were satisfied that I was emotionally stable, and competent to carry out the responsibilities of my position. During my eleven years in the district, I had never had a bad Board. I returned to my district duties. Eileen and I divorced.

I resigned from my position on June 30, 1995. I was fifty-six years old, and could have worked another ten or fifteen years. At the time, my salary was $150,000. But there was an emptiness in my heart. The Northern Highlands school Board recognized my years of leadership in a special board of education resolution. (see Appendix) An equally meaningful recognition was from the police officers with whom I had worked closely during my eleven years.

Chief Parenti and Chief Herndon were always in direct private contact with me whenever there was an issue. Officers from the APD attended my retirement dinner, and presented me with a plaque acknowledging our work for the community.

Upon reflection, my most significant achievement as superintendent was bringing NHRHS and Ho-Ho-Kus into a lasting, mutually beneficial relationship. My strategy was unconventional, as were most of my administrative initiatives. Starting with very limited knowledge of a superintendent's role, after ten years, the

New Jersey Association of School Administrators awarded me a superintendent's most prestigious honor, a Diplomate in Educational Administration. (see Appendix)

Starting Over

Our school bus vendor, Mike Ely, offered me a condo in Park Ridge to live in for as long as was necessary. I stayed there for about two months. There was not one day when I did not think of Dean. I knew that changing my geography would not change my feelings. Psychotherapy would be fruitless. I sought out a NHRHS guidance counselor, Whitey Rightmire, who lost his son in a tragic accident. He showed me his son's bedroom, with a votive candle burning. Everything was in place, as it was the last day that his son was there. For me this would be daily torture. I bought a cargo van and loaded it with my possessions. I left a lot behind, including every photograph of Dean. (Individuals have different ways of coping with a loss.)

I drove west looking for a place to live, and to start a new life. I visited Colorado, New Mexico, Texas, California, and Arizona, staying a week or two in each state. The first time I drove into Prescott, Arizona, I had a good feeling about it…Courthouse Square…Whiskey Row, antique shops, restaurants, and two casinos!

I rented a motel room, and went to a real estate office. After riding around with the realtor for three days, she showed me a house that seemed right for me. I bought it; furnished it; and moved in. A few months later, my daughter, Susan, a senior project control engineer for NASA in Pasadena, came to visit me. She introduced me to her fiancé.

The weather was great in Prescott, which has an elevation of over five thousand feet. That first winter, we got more snow than my son, Mark, got in Manhattan, where he was a client-relations manager at Moody's Investor Services. But my cold winter days were dry, which made a huge difference. I had good weather, and good neighbors.

My Website and Collections for Sale

I read an article in The Daily Courier about a new device, WebTV, whereby one could access the internet through the television. I bought one. It included a manual with instructions for setting up one's own website. It had a wireless keyboard, so I could sit and watch TV, or switch to the Internet. Having no idea what to do with my website, I simply listed some of my collections, and invited people to contact me if anything was of interest to them.

I was surprised with the reaction. A retired lawyer in Tennessee contacted me.

He said that he had a tin photograph of his deceased father, and thought that one of my daguerreotype frames might be appropriate. I described one of my best frames to him. He mailed me $300, and I mailed him the daguerreotype. Within days, a photography institution in Pittsburgh contacted me. I described my collection. The caller told me that they would be prepared to pay

$10,000-$15,000 depending on the condition of the daguerreotypes. I flew to Pittsburgh. They bought the entire collection for $15,000.

Then I received a message from a woman in North Hollywood who was interested in buying my collection of vintage photographs of nude females circa 1915–1950. When I understood that she wanted to scan them onto her business website, I rented 600 photographs to her for two weeks. She paid generously, and gave me a membership in perpetuity to her website(still active), Retro Raunch. She returned the photos, and I put them back in my collection of about two thousand photos. [Flash Forward to 2017: I sold 100 nude photos by Alexander Baege for $9,000 to a vintage photo collector in Manhattan.]

A woman in Colorado expressed interest in my buttonhook collection. She bought ten or fifteen of them. Months later, she made a surprise visit with her husband. I invited them into my living room and laid out some of my 3000 buttonhooks on a sheet on the floor. She bought $800 worth. An article that I wrote for the American Collector, Buttonhooks in America: A Reflection of Social Class, attracted several other buyers, but not enough. Currently, I am negotiating a sale with a local dealer for the remaining five hundred buttonhooks. My collection of racist Black postcards went for $5,000 to a New York City collector. He got a very good deal!

A Phone Call

One day, my ex-wife, Eileen, phoned me. She wanted to know how I was doing, what Prescott was like, and could she come for a visit? I told her that it would be okay. (journey from brooklyn) We enjoyed the visit. Soon, she sold her home in Pearl River, and joined me in Arizona!

We drove frequently to Seattle to visit her daughter, and to California to visit my daughter. Our next-door neighbor, Ron Gerber, had an antique store downtown. Whenever he went on a buying trip, Eileen would work in his antique shop. She enjoyed that. We made some friends in Chino Valley and Skull Valley.

My house, built in the 1930s, was relatively small. Eileen needed more room. I hired a builder to remove the roof and build a second level on top. The additional space included a large bedroom with a walk-in closet which I lined with cedar. The bedroom had a direct view of Thumb Butte, which we often climbed when our children visited. I had to hire a crane to lift a large outdoor hot tub and place it in back of the house. Later, I bought a house directly across the road as an investment which I rented.

Eileen and I enjoyed visiting many places: Bisbee, a historic town fifteen miles from Mexico was my favorite; Bullhead City across the Colorado River from Laughlin, Nevada; Quartzsite, the world's largest flea market; Jerome, an old mining town; and even several road trips to Puerto Penasco (Rocky Point) in Mexico.

On one of our more memorable trips to Mexico, we arranged to fly our children there for Thanksgiving dinner in a condo we had rented. Eileen prepared a feast of a dinner at home. I bought a car top carrier for $5 at a garage sale. We loaded the dinner into the carrier. Off we went to Mexico.

That night we encountered a rainstorm, and I reached up to touch our carrier, but there was nothing there. I pulled off the road, and tried to calm Eileen down. I said that we would take the kids out for dinner in Rocky Point. "No", she replied. We had to walk back in the rain and look for her dinner. She found the carrier, which was in pretty good condition. I tied it down more securely! While enjoying Thanksgiving dinner, Eileen's daughter, Melissa, crunched something in her vegetables, and removed a piece of glass from her mouth. I explained that we had a mishap enroute.

On another visit to Mexico, for some odd reason, I decided to 'test the border'. I drove onto a secondary road, and then onto a dirt road. I noticed that a helicopter appeared to be flying over our car. As I approached the Rio Grande, a border patrol vehicle cut me off in front, as a second vehicle boxed me in the rear. I answered their questions, "No, I'm not lost, I'm just curious". Then the border patrol officer called my attention to about twenty young people on a slope on the other side of the Rio Grande river. "If we were not here, they would have your wallet... your car...and maybe your life". I had satisfied my curiosity!

Eileen and I had lots of fun together, so it surprised me when she told me that she wanted to move back to New York City. Her primary reason was that there were not enough Jews in Prescott. I tried to change her thinking, mentioning the three generations of Resnicks who owned the jewelry business on Court House Square, the Navajo carpet guy, the temple on the ranch, and Zelda and Rich with their horses out in Skull Valley. I enjoyed riding with Rich. But I understood that there is something unique about Jews from Brooklyn, the Bronx, and Manhattan. Eileen was also anticipating the birth of her first grandchild in N.Y.C.

So, she went back to find a place for us. And within a month she phoned, and said that she had found the perfect co-op in Lincoln Center. I could see why she liked it. It was a corner unit on the fourteenth floor with a line of sight to Central

Park, the Empire State Building and even a peek of the Hudson River. "Will I be able to smoke?" I asked. "Yes, there is a 26' terrace". It took me two months to sell both of my Prescott properties. I moved to Lincoln Center in 2000.

Near the end of July in 2001, we were enjoying the view from the rooftop garden of my stepdaughter's condo. Holding my one- year-old granddaughter, Sarah, I pointed to the Twin Towers of the World Trade Center. On September 11 2001, I was eating breakfast while watching the TV news when I saw the plane crash into one of the towers. Eileen drove me to West 23rd Street and 10th Avenue to the Chelsea Tavern where I was scheduled to hang framed nudes on my wall inside (I had an arrangement with the owner whereby the tavern would receive a percentage of my sales (see photo). Eileen drove home. While I was refreshing the wall with new photos, the bartender hollered, "Dave, another plane just hit the other tower". Climbing down the ladder, I could see the scene on TV. I knew immediately it had to be a terrorist attack. I gathered all my photos, placed them into a shopping cart, and joined thousands of people fleeing north out of lower Manhattan. It was surreal! I walked forty- three blocks up 10th Avenue, pushing the cart of framed nudes in the heat and confusion (very odd behavior).

Building a Home on the Delaware River

Getting restless, I started looking for a house on the Delaware River. I stopped into the Penn-York Realty. They had no listings for houses on the river. However, the agent mentioned that she was going to be listing an abandoned commercial garage. We went out to see it. The garage had two long pits inside where mechanics had worked on the underside of vehicles. An official notice posted on the outside door indicated that the EPA had condemned the property. The real estate agent explained that the owner had saved the dirty oil from cars to use as heating fuel. Two of the fifty-gallon drums had rotted, seeping oil into the ground. I looked beyond that issue. (journey from brooklyn) The property was being sold 'as is'. The property itself was outstanding, with two hundred feet on the Delaware River. Across the river in **Pa., one could see only trees and cliffs.**

From the rear of the garage, there was not a house in sight, only nature. While I was prepared to bid up to $70,000, I got the

property for $25,000! Subsequently, an EPA agent visited the property, and inquired about the 'oil spill'. I told him that I had hired a man from across the river to excavate the contaminated soil. When he asked what I did with the soil, I explained that I had it trucked to an EPA approved landfill in Ohio (I had had experience with that landfill, but that would take an entire chapter). He voided the property's condemnation.

Narrowsburg is a sleepy, laid-back town. I hired a local builder, Terry Tenbus, and converted the garage into a house with four bedrooms. The old garage became a 40'x40' recreation room with a twenty-foot ceiling. One day as I drove into Narrowsburg, I was pulled over. The trooper informed me that I had just driven through a stop sign, had not signaled my right turn, and was driving 40 mph in a 30 mph zone. A few minutes later, he told me that I was driving an unregistered and uninsured vehicle!

The trooper asked me if I was a local. I replied that I owned a home on the river in the village, and that the folks at the Village Pub considered me a local. Then, recognizing the name on his shield, I mentioned that he and I had been the only two people (in a bar crowd of more than forty people) who had not dressed in costume at the Village Pub's Halloween party. (journey from brooklyn) That got his attention. I had asked Gale, the bartender, who the guy in regular clothes at the bar was, and she told me that he was the head of the state police barracks in the village, adding that he was a good guy, and that they often rode together because they were in the same bikers club.

We talked a bit, as I assured him that my car was registered and insured. He told me to put my car in neutral, go down the hill, and leave it in the St. Francis's parking lot. Three weeks later, I learned that someone had typed one incorrect digit of my VIN number on a form!!

A few years later, Marge and Gale sold the Village Pub to Richard from Paramus, N.J. He told me that his life's dream was to own a tavern in a small country town. He was a decent enough guy, but I observed that he didn't understand the local culture. The bar crowd got smaller and smaller. I stopped going to the Village Pub. Subsequently, Rich was found dead with his head on the bar. He had shot himself.

I had already moved on to the Western Hotel in Callicoon, the oldest continuously running hotel/bar in New York. This Victorian mansion dated to 1852. I enjoyed the owner, Joe, who always wore a black vest, jacket, and bow tie. However, he did a dumb thing one Saturday night after he had closed. Sitting at the bar with one of his waitresses and showing her a revolver; the gun discharged, killing the woman. Later, my son Mark and I went up for dinner. To my surprise, Joe served us. I ordered my *M*anhattan, but Joe apologized, saying that he had temporarily lost his liquor license. A few minutes later, Joe came over with a drink in a fruit juice glass, "I found some cherry juice in the kitchen". It was my *M*anhattan.

Then the floods came. The first, a 100-year flood, wiped out the ground floor of my home. I could deal with that. But the next year, we had a 500- year flood. The raging river blew out the windows on the north side of my home, crunched up the furniture in three bedrooms, and pushed out the windows on the south side. Six pickups pulled up in front of my home, unsolicited. They came in with tools, cut and removed the muddy carpeting from the 40'x40' family room. Then they removed the soaked sheetrock. After carrying all the debris to their trucks, they refused to accept any money. I asked the leader of the crew what his name was and learned that his brother was the head of the state police. The next day I went to the barracks. The lieutenant came out of his office. As I handed him six one-hundred- dollar bills, he looked up at the ceiling and said, "It's not going to look good on the videotape". He gave me his brother's address on the Flats, and said that I should just put the money under the mat at his side door. He said that he would call his brother, and tell him where to look for a surprise. I wrote a piece about this experience, The Meaning of Community, which was published in the River Reporter. (seeAppendix)

Someone once said, "you've got to know when to fold them". I listed the property at $465,000, but finally took $265,000. In 2008, the real estate market was in turmoil. With about $90,000 in the property and plenty of good times, I was satisfied. Mark still goes up to our house to fish. My wife and I visited Narrowsburg in 2017. We hooked up with my old buddy, Charlie, who lives in Narrowsburg.

On the Road Again and Another Marriage

Eileen and I had a couple of issues, which led to, "If you don't like it, get out". I moved out, and rented an apartment at 1 Main Street, Hastings-on-Hudson. I began meeting people, which was difficult at age seventy. I met a much younger woman, Magdalena, a former model from Venezuela. We got married (too quickly).

I bought a house in Boca Raton on a nice canal with an in- ground pool. We moved in. Magdalena seemed to have a large extended family, most of whom were having financial problems. I found myself sending money to Venezuela, Costa Rica, Colombia, and even $10K to her nephew, Juan, in N.J. Soon I learned that I needed abdominal surgery. At Jackson Memorial Hospital in Miami, surgeons removed some of my pancreas. At home, I was laid up, with a visiting nurse coming every day to drain the surgical site. It was clear that I would not be able to care for the property. I sold the house, and bought a condo in Miami Beach.

Then I stopped sending money to people who I had never met. I told Magdalena, "Enough of this charity stuff !" Two weeks later, Magdalena did not return home from her classes at the University of Miami, and my new car was gone.

I went to the police station in Miami Beach. The desk officer asked me who owned the car. I did, but I had put the car in both of our names. The female officer said. "She took her car". I had also stupidly put my condo in both of our names. Since my wife was homeless and unemployed, I was required to pay all of Magdalena's legal expenses, including two teams of divorce lawyers.

Soon I met Erika, but I also developed more abdominal pain. Erika drove me to Mt. Sinai Medical Center. CAT scans indicated I needed another operation. They removed more of my pancreas and my spleen. Erika visited me every day at the hospital. Finally, I got fed up with all the tests that I had over a two-week hospital stay. I phoned Erika at 2 a.m. and told her to come get me. By the time she arrived, I had disconnected my I-V lines, and cut the catheter tube off. Erika took me home. I remember trying to eat a cup of yogurt, but it wasn't going down, and the pain had gotten very bad. Apparently, one of the IVs must have been feeding me pain medicine. I went back to Mt. Sinai.

After several days of tests, Dr.Irwin came into my room. He said that I needed more surgery. He had a team ready to operate. I replied that I'd like to think it over, and let him know later. He said, "You don't have that much time. Some of your organs are beginning to lose function".

I signed the permission form. In a week or so, a rehab therapist got me up and walking. Erika took me home and moved her cats in with me. She was really good at the recovery routine.

Getting Married at Seventy-Six

Erika and I were married on September 4, 2014, at the justice of the peace's office in Miami Beach. Two office workers served as witnesses. It turned out that Erika had assumed that I would move into her home in Boca Raton; I assumed that she would move into my condo in Miami Beach. Finally, I said, "I'll sell my place; you sell your place; and we'll look for a place we both like".

I was interested in a state that did not have an income tax. We came upon Tennessee. On September 9, I saw a listing that looked too good to be true. I suggested that it would probably be a waste of time, so I would go there by myself to check it out. I flew to Charlotte and rented a car. (not knowing that one can fly to Kingsport). The realtor, Carol, and I walked the property. I whispered to her, I want to buy this property. We agreed to meet in her office at five o'clock.

When I met the realtor, she asked if I wanted to make an offer. I told her that I did. "How much do you want to offer?" I responded that the asking price was reasonable. She said that around here, buyers usually offered 10 to 15 percent less than the asking price. I had decided I did not want anyone else to get this property. I waived inspections. There would be no mortgage.I would pay full price in cash. (journey from brooklyn) I would close in thirty days. The next morning, the phone rang in my room at the Econo Lodge. It was the realtor, "Congratulations, they accepted your offer and signed the contract". When I got home to Miami Beach, I described the house and property. Erika seemed surprised that this had happened so quickly, and it was a done deal. We started packing. I went to the Oct.6th closing.

Discovering Kingsport

On October 26,2014, we drove down the steep horseshoe- shaped driveway with our suitcases and cats. After a hearty breakfast, we went home to wait for the moving trucks. One of the two trucks started down the driveway. His truck scraped the asphalt. The four moving guys managed to back the truck out.

Our next-door neighbor, Wally, came out to see what was going on. He sized up the situation, and offered to use his smaller work truck to help out. Wally drove his truck for hours into the night, with two men off-loading our stuff into Wally's truck up on Lakeside Drive, and the other two guys unloading below. They finally left at about 10 p.m. Wally would not accept any money, saying, "That's what neighbors do here".

Erika joined the Christian Women's group, the Republican Women's Club, and the Kingsport Historical Society. She is an associate member of the Daughters of the Confederacy in Johnson City, and was inducted into the Rotary Club. I obtained a Tennessee open-carry permit, and joined the Cherokee Rod and Gun Club. (see photo)

In 2015, I became concerned about our dysfunctional federal government. I wrote Transition America in which I addressed our national debt, our military deployed worldwide, the declining standards in education, health care, et al. I mailed copies of the provocative book to Donald Trump at both of his addresses. To date, the Trump administration has implemented 37 of my 61 proposals.

Building Fieldstone Walls and Other Projects

I replaced many of the property's old wooden steps with concrete ones, from the carport down to the dock, and connected the four sets of steps with concrete walkways. For me, working with concrete and mortar is like magic. I have always enjoyed building fieldstone walls.

My most famous fieldstone wall, however, I didn't build. Two industrial arts teachers were beginning a summer landscaping class, and asked me if I had any special projects. Pointing out my office window, at the deteriorated fieldstone wall that graced the entrance to our 55-acre campus at NHRHS, I said, "Every landscaper should know how to rebuild a fieldstone wall". I gave them explicit instructions: two feet wide on top and four feet wide at the base. Then I drew a cross section of a trapezoid for them to get the picture.

After a few days, the two shop teachers came to my office, and told me that the wall was done. I knew it could not possibly have been properly finished. I lost my temper, cursing at them with unpublishable language. After I calmed down, I told them to go out to the football stadium, get one of the discarded wooden bleacher seats, and an 8' construction level from the shop, and start over. They worked on it for two months. At my retirement party in 1995, the staff presented me with a framed photograph of the fieldstone wall. Nora Oliver, member of NHRHS Board of Education, had taken photographs of the wall during each of the four seasons! My cursing at those shop teachers must have reverberated throughout the building.

George Eastman founded Eastman's manufacturing site in 1920, and its global headquarters remains a critical component of Kingsport. In 1942, Holston Ordnance Works (HOW) coupled with Tennessee Eastman employed almost half of the adult population of Kingsport. One can trace a direct line from HOW's RDX/Composition B to the Y–12 facility at Oak Ridge and the Manhattan Project. This research-production line led to the rapid destruction of numerous German U-boats and the Little Boy, which was dropped on Hiroshima.

Kingsport enjoys abundant natural resources. The mountains, streams, lakes, meadows, and wooded areas are a beautiful blessing. The people are well informed, socially and politically engaged, and the friendliest that I have ever met. Actually, these characterizations remind me very much of Prescott, Az. The advantage of Kingsport, however, is its proximity to Washington, DC, Atlanta, and Charlotte, as well as the attractions and cultural richness of Virginia, Kentucky, and West Virginia.

Tennessee shares borders with eight other states: Kentucky and Virginia to the north; North Carolina to the east; Georgia, Alabama, and Mississippi to the south; Arkansas and Missouri on the Mississippi River to the west. No other state borders more states than Tennessee, and it is the only city in the United States named Kingsport!

Not counting my childhood homes, I have lived in twenty homes in half a dozen states. I'll never move from this wonderful property in this great small city of Kingsport. It has been a long and often bumpy road, but I've reached the end of my journey from Brooklyn to Kingsport.

Riding with Rich in Skull Valley

Twin Towers July 25th 2001

Refreshing My Nudes In Chelsea Tavern on 9-11!

Courier

Target Practice

AFTERWORD

Mom lived a long life. Her last forty-seven years were very good, compared to her first forty-seven years. I saw no indication that her early years had much impact on her thoughts, feelings, or happiness.

Loretta, Artie, and I enjoyed meaningful lives. Though each of us has had to cope with the psychological effects of our childhood. The deprivation, physical abuse, and absence of parental love during our developmental years had a formative impact throughout our lives.

Artie became a world-class hoarder of food, way beyond keeping a well-stocked pantry and freezer. He had a 14'x 20' addition built onto his home, which he stocked with non-perishable food.

Loretta traveled extensively. She enjoyed the fine arts and the performing arts. Yet, the fact that she never communicated with her mother for fifty-six years is indicative of the serious toll that the early years had on her.

I have had too many marriages, and attended too many universities. My street-smart Brooklyn education has served me well. I have been mistrustful, and too competitive. I see these traits and endeavors being related to my early life experiences.

And my past still lingers in the present. As recently as 2013, I happened upon a white woman being assaulted by a Black male who was on top of her. The female, bleeding from her nose, was an unwilling participant. The male had his hands around her throat, choking her. When he refused to stop, I ran to my car, retrieved my hunting knife, and plunged it into his back. I also told Magdalena to get into the drivers seat and turn the car around so that I could flee the scene in a particular direction. Had I been reared in Princeton or Cambridge, I likely would have reacted differently.

on it. Last year, I made significant contributions to good causes and good people.

Writing this memoir has been a difficult, but therapeutic experience. My purpose was to preserve a record of the anguish I endured as a child… how it affected me…and how my life transcended into one of some measure of accomplishment.

Readers may ask me any question (nothing is too personal) I will answer all. My email is: drgarrahan@gmail.com

Perhaps it is the house plants or silver lunch pail. Perhaps it is the man who has just offered you a seat. But the stark formality of what "Guidance Office" means is gone. Mr. David Garrahan has never forgotten how an unsure student feels. His warmth and casual manner eases the most troubled student. He makes human a system of subjects and tests and records, never talking a student into anything except his own dignity. No problem is ever too large or too small. Whether it be the anxiety of waiting for a college acceptance, a job after graduation, or a misunderstanding with a teacher or parent. All we can give in return for his faith in us is our faith in him. He has helped to teach us who we are, but knowing him has been the greater experience.

APPENDIX

November 25, 1996

Mr. Dave Garrahan
423 Perry Street
Prescott, Arizona 86303

Dear Mr. Garrahan,

I wanted to thank you for your very kind letter and for the military buttonhook.

Though the results on November 5th were not what we had hoped, I know that there are far worse fates than to lose an election over things you believe in. It was the honor of my life to be the Republican nominee for President of the United States, and I am very proud of the issues we raised and the solutions we proposed for the challenges facing our country.

By far the highlight of this past year was the opportunity to meet so many Americans who, like you, love our country. There is no doubt that the American people are the most generous, compassionate, and caring on the face of the earth. While I do not know exactly what the future will hold, I do know that I will continue to work for an America that is worthy of her citizens.

Please keep in touch, and let me know if I can ever be of help. Elizabeth joins with me in sending our best wishes for a happy and healthy holiday season.

Sincerely,

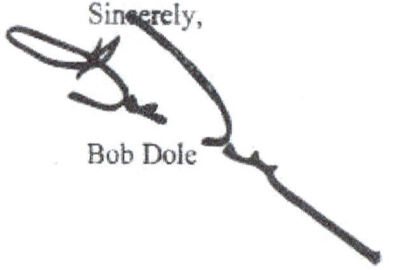

Bob Dole

SENATOR BOB DOLE
MAJORITY LEADER
U.S. SENATE

March 29, 1995

Dr. David P. Garrahan
Superintendent
Northern Highlands
298 Hillside Ave.
Allendale, NJ 07401

Dear Dr. Garrahan,

After meeting with RNC Chairman Haley Barbour and his nominating committee, I am pleased to inform you that you have been recommended for membership on the Chairman's Advisory Board, one of the most effective and influential senior leadership councils within the national Republican Party.

The Chairman's Advisory Board offers a unique opportunity for you to participate personally in the development of Republican policy positions and campaign strategies at the highest levels of the Party.

Meeting regularly with a mix of business and social sessions, the Board's small and highly selective membership permits informal and collegial discussion of political and policy questions among its members and guests, who regularly include Republican Congressional leaders, governors, Presidential candidates, and the national Party leadership.

These conversations will be instrumental not only helping to chart Republican strategy in the current Congress but the results of these meetings will also be presented to the 1996 Republican Convention Platform Committee.

The Spring meeting of the Chairman's Advisory Board will be held May 10-11, 1995 in Washington, D.C. The new Republican leadership of the U.S. Senate and House of Representatives will be featured guests.

In the near future, Republican National Committee Chairman Haley Barbour will be sending you a formal invitation to join the Chairman's Advisory Board and reservation materials for the Spring meeting. I congratulate you on your nomination, and I look forward to personally welcoming you to the Board in May.

Sincerely,

Bob Dole

PAID FOR BY THE REPUBLICAN NATIONAL COMMITTEE
NOT PRINTED AT GOVERNMENT EXPENSE

Columbia University
in the City of New York

NEW YORK, N.Y. 10027

PRESIDENT'S ROOM

February 3, 1972

Dear Mr. Garrahan:

I have your letter of January twenty-eighth and want to begin my reply by thanking you for the courteous way in which you have raised an extremely sensitive topic.

I am enclosing a copy of our explanation of the situation involving anticipated lay-offs of maids at the University. We are operating under a serious constraint because we have signed a contract with the Transport Workers Union which contains explicit seniority provisions and a hierarchy of job titles. Thus, when we seek to bring our work force within budgeted limits, we must conform to the terms of the contract. Such constraints led us to an action where we find it difficult to explain and which we would not take if we were operating on our own discretion.

I find it difficult to follow your reasoning about our deficit. We construct a budget and we are obliged to live within it. Otherwise there is no hope for dealing with our fiscal problems. Our budget anticipates a certain staff and we need to try to achieve it. Any particular failure is trivial, but any failure to enforce the budget immediately suggests that we fail everywhere. The reasoning is elementary and I am sure you see it. No part of the University bureaucracy is able to accept budget cuts aimed uniquely at them.

We are doing our best to address ourselves to every problem we confront. There is no issue large or small at Columbia that would not be materially improved by $50 million, but we do not have it.

Sincerely,

William J. McGill
President

136 APPLIED HUMAN DEVELOPMENT AND GUIDANCE

TG3502. Community agencies and resources (2 or 3)
MRS. BYNUM: Autumn M 5:10-6:50.
Designed to familiarize students with community social services agencies functioning in the areas of family service, public assistance, mental health, recreational, protective and correctional care, gerontological service, employment, and vocational guidance. Field visits in small groups.

T13502. Human ecology (3)
PROFESSOR GRANNIS: Autumn Th 7:20-9 p.m.
Analysis of theory and research on the interaction of physical, social, and psychological factors in the settings of human behavior. Focus on the ecological problems of political, economic, educational, or health intervention in community and institutional settings.

T13503. Ecological observation for intervention (3)
PROFESSOR BROK: Spring Th 5:10-6:50.
Application of ecological observation techniques to community and institutional behavior settings for purposes of designing interventions. Training in behavior stream observation, behavior setting observation, and milieu description, with particular emphasis on the location of causality in the settings observed: classrooms, hospital wards, street corner gatherings, etc.

TG3510. Field work in applied human development (2)
MRS. BYNUM (Sec 1), HTBA (Sec 2): Autumn HTBA.
Guided observation in selected human development settings such as schools, agencies, nursing homes, etc. Individual and group conferences with staff.

TG4011. Multidisciplinary research in the service of human development (2)
PROFESSOR MORRIS: Autumn W 5:10-6:50.
Basic concepts and techniques for the conduct of simple research studies and the utilization of research findings from the literature which can be useful in improving practice and persuading others.

TG4110. Implications of bio-social differences for guiding human development (2 or 3)
PROFESSOR GORDON: Spring Th 3-4:40.
Seminar on the nature and meaning of bio-social differences. Review of contemporary conceptions, issues and research concerning such aspects of human diversity as age, cognitive style, ethnicity, sex, and social context. Theoretical and practical implications for applied human development.

TG4111. Educational and vocational implications of ethnic and social status differences (2 or 3)
PROFESSOR GARRAHAN: Spring M 5:10-6:50.
The relationship of economic, ethnic, and social status differences to educational and vocational opportunities and advancement. Implications for educational and career development.

OFFICE OF THE REGISTRAR
TEACHERS COLLEGE · COLUMBIA UNIVERSITY
NEW YORK, N.Y. 10027
GRADE REPORT

SEM.	YEAR	ACAD. STATUS	MAJOR FIELD	STUDENT NUMBER
2	70	97	TGS	N06240

SPRING, 1970

COURSE NO.	POINTS	GRADE	COURSE TITLE
T15831	2	P	TECH COLLCTN & ORG OF EVIDENCE
T13802	3	A+	STATISTICAL INFERENCE
T68913	4	P	RESEARCH IN GUIDANCE
TF3100	3	R	ANTHROPOLOGY & EDUCATION

* GRADES HAVE NOT YET BEEN RECEIVED FOR THESE POINTS

STUDENT COPY

STUDENT NAME: MR DAVID GARRAHAN
3618 TIBBETT AVE
BRONX N Y 10463

I have known David P. Garrahan for five years as a colleague in a closely related department and have come to hold him in the highest regard. It is my strong hope that he remain at T.C. and were he to do so, I would readily accept him as a member of the Department of Psychology Faculty.

Dr. Garrahan is extremely bright, exceedingly well-prepared, and possessed of an energy level that sometimes makes us mere mortals shutter. He is a superb teacher, and excellent clear writer, and a mature and dedicated adviser to graduate students. He has an astute sense about applied psychological research which he shares quickly and easily with students.

Most important of all, Dr. Garrahan is one of those whose work style illustrates the meaning of interdependence. Capable of outstanding individual work, he is also among the best I've seen at functioning in cooperative ventures. He has a kind of professional selflessness that I consider essential to the academy at this time.

To any who seek the very best of professors in guidance and counseling I suggest: you would be enriched by association with David Garrahan.

Roger A. Myers

Teachers College, Columbia Univ.

March 22, 1977
Professor and Chairman of the
Department of Psychology & Education

525 W. 120 St., New York, NY 10027

We appreciate your evaluation of the registrant whose name appears below, referring to such factors as scholarship, ability, experience and professional promise. Please do not refer to race, color, creed, national origin or age.

PLEASE LIMIT COMMENTS TO THIS SINGLE PAGE.

CONFIDENTIAL and to be sent directly to: Office of Placement, Teachers College, Columbia University, 525 West 120th Street, New York, New York 10027

Concerning: David P. Garrahan

I have known Dave Garrahan for about eight years. During this period he was initially a student of mine, later a part of my research staff and for the past five years as a faculty colleague. He is a highly intelligent person who brings thoroughness, initiative and sensitivity to bear on his work. He has a high sense of professional responsibility and tends to be oriented more toward scholarly practice than toward investigative research. He is thoughtful about his work. He reads widely. He is self-critical. As a teacher he brings his conscientiousness and deep sensitivity to the social relevance of his profession to the classroom. He is demanding yet compassionate with his students. He richly integrates his wide experience in education with an excellent mastery of the dominant currents of his profession. I am suggesting that Dave is not a discipline-based person but a scholar rooted in the application of behavioral science disciplines to the profession we call guidance and student development. In this role he is highly regarded by his students and colleagues. He is actively sought as an advisor by students. His colleagues at the College and in his profession readily turn to him for leadership. He can be depended on to bring wisdom and realism to bear on complex problems.

Signature: [signed]

Date: Feb. 14, 1977

Director, Inst. for Urb. & Min. Ed.

Edmund W. Gordon
Teachers College, Columbia University

Professor, Dept. of Appl. Hum. Dev. & Guid.

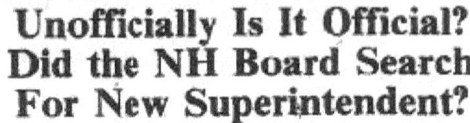

Trustee Confirms Motion To Name Dr. Garrahan NHRHS Superintendent

Other Trustees Mum on Subject

selection process. Mr. Arnold is the best person to confirm or deny any statements." Mr. Hopkins, when asked who made up the membership of the Search Committee, said he thought it consisted of Mr. Arnold, Trustee Terry Bolles, Mrs. Aiuvalasit...

Trustee appointment stirs legal dispute

D-10   THE RECORD, TUESDAY, MARCH 12, 1985   BERGEN

Affirmative-action issue raised by appointment

Unofficially Is It Official? Did the NH Board Search For New Superintendent?

Vol. 11, No. 44   Entered as Second Class at Saddle River, N.J.

It's Official: Dr. Ga... NH Su...

Large Crowd Opposes Selection Process

Foreign trips banned indefinite

By Jennifer Klein

In a memo issued to all foreign language teachers on March 11, superintendent Dr. David Garrahan "banned" all foreign trips originating at the school effective July 1986. This action was prompted by "a combination of factors," according to Dr. Garrahan. "I have received governmental literature from a concerned parent who works for an airline that suggests cutting foreign travel." Due to the recent terrorist activities in Europe, the destination of the trips affected by this ban, and the "irrational nature" of Moammar Quadaffi of Libya who has threatened to target [our] children", Dr. Garrahan decided to place restrictions on all future trips. The decision, he says "was not a Board decision. It is mine. It was intended to put a serious nature of these [terrorist] incidents in perspective." The memo stressed the restriction of foreign travel "as a group" and thus it does not affect travel with AFS or study travel programs. "I place these in a different category as they usually don't involve large groups of students.", according to the Superintendent.

Dr. Garrahan also expressed concern due to rising insurance and liability rates. "Since last year, our insurance rates have gone up 182%." He cited a recent legal ruling in which a school was sued by parents of a student who was injured while on a trip originating at the school. "Although the school did not actually sponsor the trip, the students and teachers involved were from the school and promotional literature was posted in the school." Mrs. Rosemarie Mastropoulo had planned a trip to Italy and Greece for her Latin students, but due to the airport bombings in Rome and Athens, two of their principal destinations, 6 of the 10 participants withdrew. "We thought that it would be smart to go.", says Mrs. Mastropoulo.

Mr. Stephen Murray, though, did not cancel his students trip to Germany because of terrorist activity, but rather because it was "a question of finance." The cost has become too high for many students to afford.

Dr. Garrahan's concern for this...

On March 11, 1986, our Superintendent, Dr. David P. Garrahan, issued a memo to all the foreign language teachers, advising them to cancel their trips with students abroad (e.g. Mr. Gilli's trip to France, Mrs. Mastropoulo's trip to Italy and Greece) during the spring break. He issued this memo because of the "probability of danger as a result of terrorist activity" which was expressed in information that he received from certain government agencies. Dr. Garrahan also banned future student trips to foreign countries as of July 1, 1986. I asked Dr. Garrahan if this was his decision or the Board of Education's decision, it was his.

The ban states that the Northern Highlands School District will not sponsor, support, or encourage in any manner foreign trips by students. It prohibits the distribution of literature relating to student tours in the building and states that no literature will be posted in the classrooms. The ban forbids the discussion of foreign trips with students on school property as well.

One issue that Dr. Garrahan has is the probable danger resulting from terrorist activity in foreign countries. In today's world, terrorist activity is possible, not probable, at anytime, anywhere. It is uncomfortable. Terrorism can occur just as easily in New York City as it can in any other city in the world (it could even occur to Dr. Garrahan's unclaimed office). Does this mean that we should cancel our field trips to the Metropolitan Museum of Art? Or to the high school office? Does this mean that we should assume that terrorist activity will be a threat to us wherever we go?

Perhaps Dr. Garrahan is worried that the school will be held liable for any injuries that may occur to the students while on these trips. However, these tours are taken during the spring vacation, school is closed. The only connection these student tours have with the school is that both the students and the teachers go to the school. Students and their parents sign a document with the companies that run these tours that hold the parents responsible for any "accidents" over which the company has no control. On top of this, the companies carry insurance policies on each student and indemnify the schools.

The school is a meeting place. Most of the students and the faculty spend more than nine hours a day here. By placing a ban on student trips, Dr. Garrahan has made organizing a trip abroad extremely difficult, almost impossible. The Northern Highlands School District has never sponsored, supported, or encouraged these trips in the first place. The students and the teachers have cooperated to arrange all twenty of the past trips on their own time. Furthermore, what purpose could restricting even conversation about these trips possibly serve? Aside from being anti-educational, this seems to violate

Leaching life blood from foreign travel

Union's demand quashes deal
NH board yanks 8-period day

Suzan Erem

NORTHERN HIGHLANDS — In response to demands from the Northern Highlands Education Association to negotiate implementation of the eight-period day, school board president Jim Ryan Feb. 1 rescinded the board's approval of the proposal.

Guidance counselors began scheduling

negotiate the implementation thereof..." the resolution stated.

Association President Pat Al-Arnasi, acting on advice from an association attorney, recommended to her membership that any changes in working conditions — such as duties assigned during the eighth period — be negotiated.

$20 Yearly, 45¢ Single Copy   Thursday, November 14, 1991

At NH meeting:
Talk but no action on 8-period day impasse

Dan Skelton, Jr.

NORTHERN HIGHLANDS — The board of education closed the high school Nov. 11 due to the walkout of Education Association members who were protesting the impasse in their negotiations with the board for a 1991-92 contract. Negotiations are stalled over the issue of a sixth teaching period that the board wishes to add for an eight-period schedule.

said that he was in favor of the eight-period day, and that it is unfortunate that Highlands did not begin working on such a schedule in 1989 when the board and the faculty last discussed it. When Mr. Larsen specifically asked Superintendent Garrahan if he thought the additional sixth period would affect the teachers' performance, Dr. Garrahan replied, "It's

Attention - Citizens of Allendale & Upper Saddle River

There is a crisis at Northern Highlands Regional High School. The underlying reason for this crisis is that Superintendent David Garrahan, in partnership with the Board of Education, has failed to provide the school community with sound educational leadership. Therefore, a resolution has been passed by the Northern Highlands Education Association:

Whereas:

Superintendent Garrahan has neglected to organize a democratic coalition of students, parents, teachers and administrators to closely examine the current and future needs of the school, and to determine how the resources of the district can be used wisely and impartially for the greatest benefit of all students, and

Whereas:

Superintendent Garrahan has made contradictory statements regarding his own position on vital school matters thereby contributing to confusion and misunderstanding within the school community, and

Whereas:

Superintendent Garrahan has failed to encourage and maintain an atmosphere of mutual trust and respect once characteristic of Northern Highlands,

Therefore:

The members of the Northern Highlands Education Association have taken a vote of **No Confidence** in Superintendent Garrahan.

NORTHERN HIGHLANDS EDUCATION ASSOCIATION

by Northern Highlands Education Association, Pat Cline, president

After 43 years on the force Chief Parenti says, 'I love the people'

THE HIGHLANDS REPORT

Northern Highlands Regional High School District • Allendale/Upper Saddle River, N.J. December 1993

Highlands Achieves National Recognition

The United States Department of Education's Drug-Free School Recognition Program acknowledges schools that have worked to achieve safe, disciplined, drug-free environments. Northern Highlands was one of only twenty public high schools nationwide to receive this highest distinction and was honored at a ceremony at the Capitol. Superintendent Garrahan and Vince Herold, Principal, accepted the award for Highlands during a two day visit to the White House in September. Dr. Garrahan recalled that "The ceremonial events were eclipsed because of the sudden and dramatic Mideast Peace Treaty. The awards program was to have been in the Rose Garden, with President Clinton in attendance. As it turned out, Yasser Arafat's motorcade passed in front of our bus as he headed for the signing of the agreement at the White House - and the honorees were re-routed to the Georgetown University Campus."

In presenting the awards, Secretary of Education Richard Riley commented that "These schools survived a very rigorous review process and are deserving of the award." The process began in October, 1992, when the District filed a 27 page application detailing its substance use prevention program and documented its effectiveness.

A panel of State health and education officials reviewed all applications, and Highlands was nominated to the U.S. Department of Education. After further screening, we were selected for an on-site visit in March, 1993, and finally, in June we learned that we had been selected for this honor. It is interesting to note that from within the Northeast Region Center for Drug-free Schools and Communities, which extends from Maryland to Maine, and west to Ohio, there was only one other high school recognized - Whippany Park High School in New Jersey.

Winning schools had to successfully address all six of the criteria for a drug-free school:

--recognizing, assessing, and monitoring of the problem
--setting, implementing, and enforcing policy
--developing and implementing a drug education and prevention program
--educating and training staff
--promoting parent involvement and providing parent education and training, and
--interacting and networking with community groups and agencies.

Senator Orrin Hatch congratulates Dr. Garrahan

Is it student piracy, or fair competition?
N. Highlands woos non-residents

Schools can set property value
Reading, 'riting, and reputation

NH 'offers better product at better price'

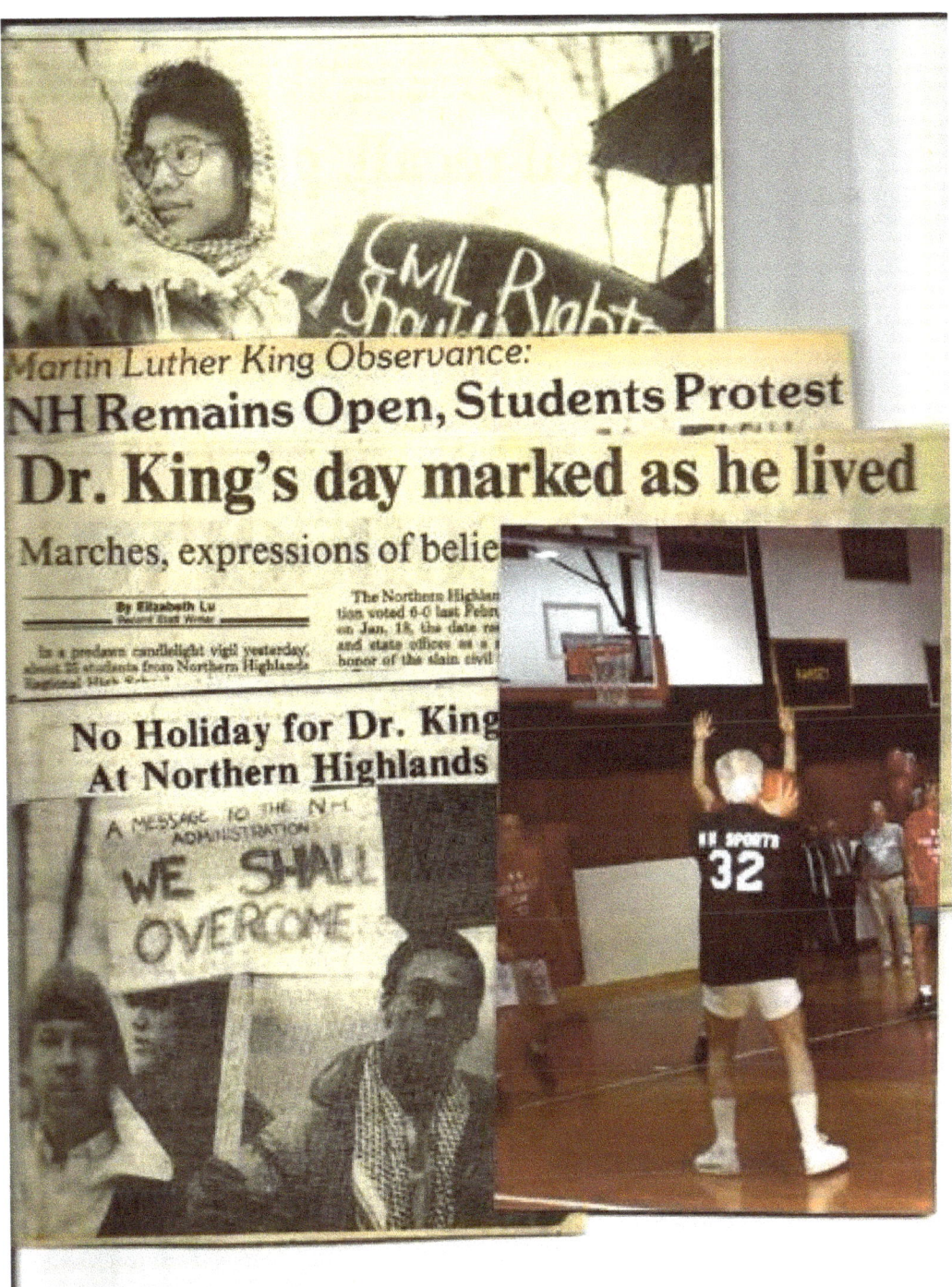

Referred to consultants' work as "legalized hit-and-run."

Jack Mintzer
NH principal

"The report calls for a redeployment of existing personnel."

Dr. David Garrahan
Supt. of NH

Despite gains in NH stature, staff and supt. divided

Faculty critical of Savitt report

Mary Service

NORTHERN HIGHLANDS — When the board of education commissioned a study of the administrative structure of the high school last fall, it undoubtedly did not expect Al Vinci, the recently retired vice principal, to declare, "You're going to tear down the school and ruin morale." But that was one of many negative comments when the Savitt report was discussed in the school library Feb. 13 at the board of education meeting.

That evening Dr. Robert Savitt, president of Guidelines, Inc., which prepared

(Continued on page 8)

Light is cast on resignation of principal

N. Highlands crowd riveted

By CHARLES SAYDAH
Staff Writer

ALLENDALE — During an emotional Northern Highlands Board of Education meeting Monday night, the silence surrounding the resignation of the school's popular principal started dissolving.

Former board President James Ryan of Allendale cast some of the strongest light on the resignation of Geoffrey Gordon, the 46-year-old principal whom students and parents had credited with restoring spirit in the 685-student school.

His brief statement riveted more than 50 people still left in the school library two hours after the discussion about Gordon's resignation began. Ryan hinted at some aspects of the affair that had never been considered.

"The board knows very well that they did not have to accept Dr. Gordon's resignation," Ryan said. "But the fact is that nine out of nine accepted it."

don's action, and on the board for acquiescing. The board said it would set up a committee to hire a search firm, which would select five candidates to be considered by the board.

Despite the light Ryan shed on the inner workings of the board, spectators who left the meeting a half-hour earlier had few concrete answers to explain why Gordon will leave on June 30.

As for Gordon's departure, board attorney Jamie Plosia said a gag order signed by both Gordon and the board prohibits any discussion. No school official or board member will say anything concerning Gordon's job performance. Gordon will not say whether it was a personality conflict with Garrahan that caused him to resign.

In addition, Garrahan and board members will say nothing derogatory or negative about Gordon; Gordon will say nothing derogatory or negative about Garrahan or the Northern Highlands Regional School District. In ex-

Code of silence in principal's ouster

By PAUL DAVIDSON

ALLENDALE — A former official of Northern Highlands Regional High School believes the school district's controversial recommendation not to retain the school's well-liked principal was not sparked by a glaring wrongdoing or personality clash.

The official, who requested anonymity, said there is an erroneous public perception that Principal Geoffrey Gordon may have committed a malfeasance or locked horns with Schools Superintendent David Garrahan.

Rather, the source thinks the decision was based on an evaluation of Geoffrey Gordon's "behind-the-scenes" adminis-

trative performance at the school, which serves 685 students from Allendale and Upper Saddle River. The source would not elaborate.

Citing an agreement binding all parties to vows of silence, Gordon, Garrahan and board of education members have refused to discuss the reasons for the resignation, fueling public speculation and rumors.

Since taking the job last July, the 46-year-old Gordon has been praised by parents for his dealings with students and for restoring school spirit after a long teacher contract dispute.

"What they don't see is what goes on behind the scenes," the former school official said.

(See PRINCIPAL, page 4)

"So take your anger out on me," he said, referring to the strong support expressed for Gordon by parents and students. Much of it came as virulent denunciations of Garrahan, who was portrayed as the villain in a melodrama fabricated by rumor and inference as well as hard facts.

That task involved designing the process to find Gordon's successor, the item that started the audience of 110 on its dual attack — on Garrahan for forcing Gor-

Garrahan had tried to end the public discussion at about 11 p.m. "This is precisely what Dr. Gordon and I did not want to happen tonight," he said, characterizing some of the remarks made about him as offensive and libelous.

But Ryan had the last word

"Dr. Garrahan has served the board well, and in my opinion the board has served the people well," he said, his voice shaky. "All the board members are like the people you know."

Dr. Gordon resigns as NH principal

Principal stuns crowd, resigns Highlands post

Principal resigns
Students are not a pri[ority]

Light is cast on resignation of principal

Highlands students demanding answers

Why did popular principal resign

N. Highlands crowd riveted

Principal's resignation opposed

Code of silence in principal's ouster

popular principal resigns

Unaswered questions spark student/parent protests

By Colleen Herndon

Approximately 200 people attended Monday night's board meeting in order to show their support for former principal Dr. Geoffrey Gordon, and to question what method would be used to choose his successor.

Two weeks before, in an emotional statement given at the Board of Education's May 10 work session, Dr. Gordon said that he tendered his resignation "with regret." Approximately 70 people, mostly parents and students with a want this discussed in public," said Board of Education President Marcie Aiuvalasit. Mr. Vince Herold, vice-principal, declined to discuss the resignation at this time because of the legal ramifications and because Dr. Gordon requested that no comment be made.

Teachers, parents, and students remain in the dark about the reasons behind Dr. Gordon's resignation. One rumor was that Dr. Gordon did not get along with Dr. David Garrahan, Superintendent. According to the May 10 issue of the Town Journal, the terms of the resignation Agreement and Release listed in the agreement that would suggest Dr. Gordon was given money by the Board to resign.

A separate two page release signed by Dr. Gordon states that he "had adequate opportunity to review his release" as well as ". . . opportunity to consult with an attorney." There has yet to be any discussion of who the Board will hire to replace Gordon, and several students said that finding a match for him will be difficult. Junior Darrell Drason states, "The next principal we have is not going to be welcomed by faculty or students because we all feel that Dr. Gordon was an

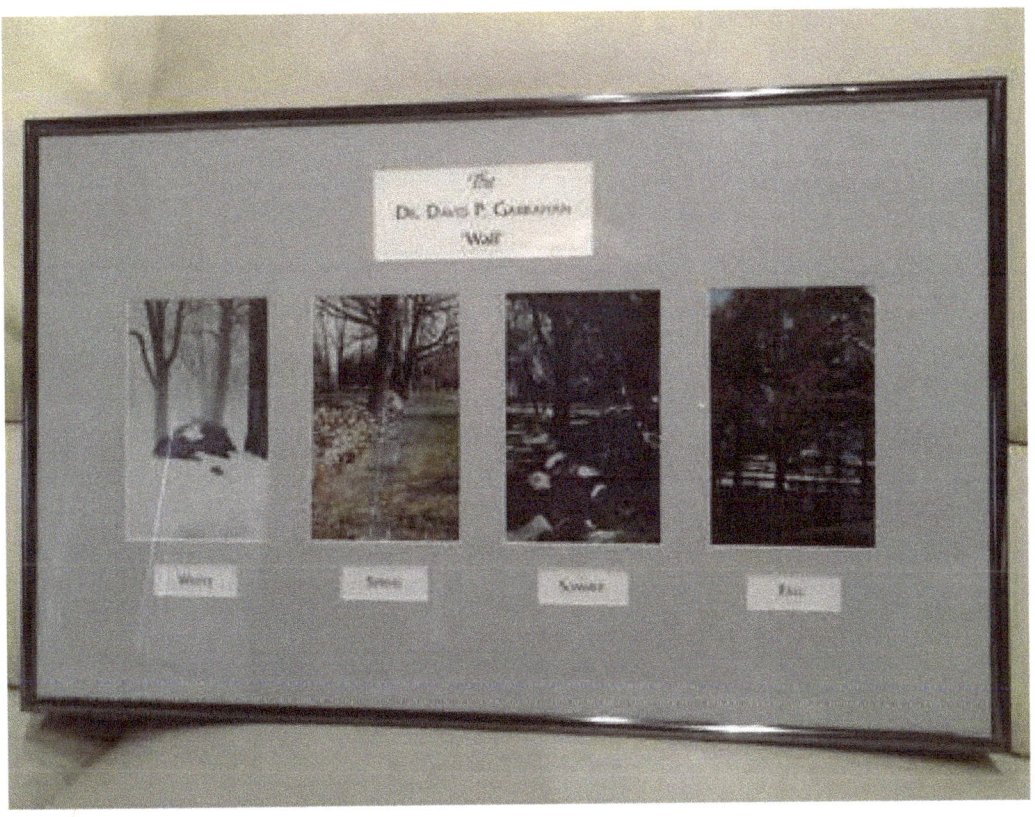

State of New Jersey
DEPARTMENT OF EDUCATION
BERGEN COUNTY OFFICE OF EDUCATION
327 E. RIDGEWOOD AVENUE
PARAMUS, NEW JERSEY 07652
(201) 599-6256
(201) 599-6255 FAX

M. RAY KELLY
COUNTY SUPERINTENDENT

JOHN ELLIS
COMMISSIONER

RESOLUTION

WHEREAS, Dr. David P. Garrahan has had a distinguished career in education; and

WHEREAS, he has consistently exemplified the characteristics of an outstanding educational leader; and

WHEREAS, his leadership has extended throughout the Northern Highlands Regional High School District by serving as Superintendent of Schools; and

WHEREAS, Dr. David P. Garrahan has demonstrated superior professional skills, and a strong commitment to the well-being of students, teachers, staff members, colleagues, and parents:

NOW, THEREFORE

BE IT HEREBY RESOLVED, that Dr. David P. Garrahan be recognized as a "Distinguished Educator" by the Bergen County Superintendent of Schools on this date, June 28, 1991.

BERGEN COUNTY SUPERINTENDENT OF SCHOOLS

New Jersey Association of School Administrators

920 West State Street, Trenton, New Jersey 08618
Telephone: (609) 599-2900/Fax: (609) 599-1893

April 12, 1994

Dr. David P. Garrahan
Superintendent of Schools
Northern Highlands Regional High School District
Hillside Avenue
Allendale, New Jersey 07401

Dear David:

It is my pleasure to inform you, on behalf of the NJASA Officers, Executive Committee, and Diplomate Committee, that you have been officially designated as an NJASA Diplomate in Educational Administration.

The Diplomate Review Committee found that your candidacy reflected the highest standards of professional performance, career commitment and scholarly contributions to education.

Your distinguished professional career will be honored at the NJASA/NJSBA Spring Conference on Sunday, May 22, 1994, at the NJASA Leadership Brunch scheduled for 11:30 a.m. to 1:30 p.m., where your Diplomate certificate will be conferred. Please let us know if you will attend.

Also, we would be most pleased to send a press release regarding your achievement of the Diplomate to two newspapers of your choice. Simply designate (in writing) the newspaper name, address and contact person and we will send the press release immediately.

Again, our warmest congratulations on your attainment of this award.

Sincerely,

Harriett

Harriett S. Thomas, CAE
Assistant Executive Director

HST:nhw

DIPLOMATE

In School Administration

To all persons to whom these presents may come,

Greetings:

Be it known that

David P. Garrahan

In recognition of career performance as a school administrator in New Jersey, and validated by a systematic assessment and analysis of professional attainment through a rigorous process of peer review.

This Diplomate has been earned and, therefore, is so conferred by the New Jersey Association of School Administrators in the State capital of Trenton. The **22nd** day of **May 1994**. This Diplomate in School Administration satisfies the professional requirements as decreed by this professional association.

RESUME

David Garrahan
160 West End Ave.
New York, N.Y. 10023

East Stroudsburg State College	1961	B.S. (Mathematics, Science)
Lehigh University	1963	M.Ed. (Guidance, Counseling)
Columbia University	1972	Ed.D. (Psychological Counseling)
Rutgers - The State University	1963	Guidance & Counseling Institute
Cornell University, New York Univ., Univ. of Scranton	1961-67	Additional Graduate Study
Institute for Advanced Study of Rational Psychotherapy	1974	Certificate (Clinical Supervision by Albert Ellis)
Transactional Analysis	1984	Certificate
School Executive Academy	1985	Program Certificate
Harvard University	1990	Current Issues in School Law Institute
NJ Assn. of School Administrators	1994	Diplomate in Educational Administration

PROFESSIONAL EXPERIENCE

1985-1995	Northern Highlands Regional High School District	District Superintendent
1984-1985	Northern Highlands Regional High School District	Director of Pupil Personnel Services
1982-1984	Teaneck High School (N.J)	Director of Guidance
1978-1982	Pascack Valley H.S. (NJ)	Guidance Counselor

2.

1977-1978	Frostburg State College (MD)	Associate Professor of Psychology and Director of Graduate Programs in Counseling, Psychology, and Guidance
1975-1977	Teachers College Columbia University	Assistant Professor of Education and Coordinator of Masters and Doctoral Guidance Programs and Clinical Associate Psychological Consultation Ctr.
1974-1975	Teachers College Columbia University	Deputy Chairman - Dept. of Human Development (Gerontology, Guidance, and Leisure Education)
1972-1974	Teachers College Columbia University	Assistant Professor of Education and Coordinator of Elementary and Secondary Guidance Programs
1969-1972	Teachers College Columbia University	Instructor and Research Associate
1963-1969	Washingtonville High School (NY)	Guidance Counselor
1961-1963	Belvidere High School (NJ)	Teacher (Mathematics and Science)

PROFESSIONAL CONSULTING

Bridgewater-Raritan Regional School District (NJ)	1988	In-service: Back to the Future - A View from the Top
Watchung Hills Regional High School (NJ)	1986	Responding to Community Expectations
Bloomfield Public Schools (NJ)	1985	Needs Assessment Program Evaluation

3.

Airco Corporation - Computer Learning Center Division	1984	Staff Development and Training
New York City Board of Education	1980-82	Grant Proposal Writer
New York City Board of Education	1979	Operation FAR CRY: Training Consultant
New York City Board of Education	1979	Administrator of School Security Officer Program
Vaslock Corporation (NYC)	1978-82	Management Consultant: Market Research; Personnel Training; Publications
Eastern Technical School, Inc. (NYC)	1978-82	Consulting Director of Educational Services
New York City Board of Education	1978	Staff Development - Auxiliary Services for High School
New York City Board of Education	1978	Consultant to the President of the Board of Education
Eastern School for Physicians Aides, Inc. (NYC)	1977-78	Liaison to State Education Services Department and Accrediting Agencies
Institute of Gerontology College of Misericordia (PA)	1977	Nursing Home Administrator - Training Workshops
Ridgefield Park High School (NJ)	1977	School Community Needs Assessment
Metuchen High School (NJ)	1977	Elementary Guidance: Behavior Modification Techniques for Teachers
Delehanty Institute, Inc. (NYC)	1976-78	Grant Proposal Writer and Federal Projects Coordinator
Watchung Hills Regional High School (NJ)	1976	Series of In-service Staff Development Seminars

Hastings-on-Hudson School District (NY)	1976	Pupil Personnel Services (K-12) Five-Year Reorganization Plan
Institute for Human Development, Resource Development Associates, Inc. (NJ)	1975-76	Fund-raising; Grants; Seminars
Greenburgh Central School (NY)	1975	Evaluation of Professional Personnel
Teaneck School District (NJ)	1974	Evaluation of District Guidance Services
Great Neck Public Schools (NY)	1974	Reorganizing Guidance Services
New York City Bd. of Ed.	1971-74	Member - Board of Examiners
Norwalk Public Schools (CT)	1973	Third Party Evaluation - U.S.O.E. Career Education
Leonia High School (NJ)	1973	Guidance Program: Evaluation
Hackensack High School (NJ)	1972	Career Education: In-service Training
New York State Education Department	1972	Guidance Study Kit: Research and Development
Glen Rock High School (NJ)	1971	Reconceptualizing Guidance: In-service Workshop

PUBLICATIONS AND RESEARCH REPORTS

Garrahan, D. The Application of a Systems Approach to Substance Use Prevention: Linking Interventions to the Infrastructure. Journal of Alcohol and Drug Education, Vol. 40, No. 3, pp. 74-83, Spring 1995.

Garrahan, D. and Plosia, J. Time's Up for Teacher Tenure. New Jersey Reporter, Vol. 25, No. 1, pp. 8-9, May/June 1995.

Garrahan, D. and Plosia, J. Time's Up for Tenure: A Plan for a Better System (reprint). The Press (Atlantic City), p. A-11, June 28, 1995.

Books:
D. Garrahan, Transition America, 2016
D. Garrahan, From Brooklyn To Kingsport, 2018
D. Garrahan, Brooklyn Bred, 2019

5.

Garrahan, D. A Bold New Reform for the Year 2000. The Record, Vol. 101, No. 14, p. 10, June 20, 1995.

Garrahan, D. Healing a "Sick" System: Disjointed Education Reform Efforts Need the Salve of Unity to Succeed. School Leader, Vol. 24, No. 5, pp. 32-34, 50, March/April 1995.

Garrahan, D. Spotlighting: Northern Highlands Regional High School. The Northwest News, Vol. 3, No. 11, p. 11, November 1994.

Garrahan, D. Military Tradition: African-Americans in Military Service. Barr's News, Vol. 20, pp. 1 and 68, October 3, 1994.

Garrahan, D. Education's Most Sacred Cow. School Leader, Vol. 24, No. 1, pp. 27-29, 42-43, July/August 1994.

Garrahan, D. Buttonhooks in America: A Reflection of Social Class (Reprint). The American Collector, Vol. 24, No. 1, pp. 10-11, March 1994.

Garrahan, D. Cancelled Cards Document Racism In American Social History. Postcard Collector, Vol. 11, No. 8, pp. 51-53, August 1993.

Garrahan, D. School Board Reform: The Case for Redefining the Role of Lay Governance in Public Education. Perspective, Vol. 10, No. 1, pp. 4-10, Spring 1993.

Garrahan, D. Regionalization - Sensible Strategy or Quick Fix? Point-Counterpoint article. School Leader, Vol. 21, No. 5, pp. 38-39 and 46-47, March/April, 1992.

Garrahan, D. Regionalization and the Organizational Transformation of Education. Perspective, Vol. 8, No. 4, pp. 27-31, Winter, 1992.

Garrahan, D. School Regionalization Makes Sense. Commentary. New Jersey Reporter, Vol. 21, No. 3, pp. 39 and 45, September/October, 1991.

Garrahan, D. Superintendent Opposed to Tenure. The Town Journal, Vol.18, No. 3, p. 3, May 16, 1991.

Garrahan, D. Monitoring and School Deregulation. School Leader, Vol. 19, No. 6, pp. 26-29, 43, May/June, 1990.

Garrahan, D. Implementing a School Security Program. Perspective, Vol. VI, No. 1, pp. 13-14, Spring 1989.

Garrahan, D. and Simeonicis, M. Partners in Education: Tots, Teens, and Parents. School Leader, Vol. 17, No. 7, pp. 36-48, September/October 1988.

Garrahan, D. Buttonhooks in America: A Reflection of Social Class. The Antique Trader, pp. 102-103, October 1986.

Garrahan, D. Gerontological Counseling: A Developmental Life Stage Approach. N. J. Journal of Professional Counseling, Vol. 49, No. 1, pp. 4-6, Spring, 1986.

Garrahan, D. Administering a Needs Assessment Evaluation of Student Services. Perspective, Vol. 3, No. 4, pp. 12-13, 35-36, Fall/Winter, 1985.

Garrahan, D. Guidance Evaluation. Bloomfield, NJ, Public Schools, 115 pages, June, 1985.

Garrahan, D. College Admissions Experience Profile: Development and Implementation (Cassette tape). Instant Replay Services, Inc., Arlington, VA, October, 1984.

Garrahan, D. Cargo Security: Moving Out of the Dark Ages. Enroute, Vol.12, No. 5, pp. 18-19, May 30, 1982.

Garrahan, D. Vaslock Training Manual. Vollmer Auto Security Corporation, New York, 57 pages, May, 1981.

Garrahan, D. Guidance and Counseling Internship Guide. Frostburg State College, Maryland, 27 pages, 1978.

Garrahan, D. and Stewart, K. Counseling Psychology Internship Guide. Frostburg State College, Maryland, 12 pages, 1977.

Garrahan, D. Employment, Economic Conditions, and Adaptability. Delehanty Digest, Vol. 1, No. 4, November, 1977.

Garrahan, D. Evaluative Self-Study. Teaneck, NJ, 36 pages, June, 1974.

Garrahan, D. The Relationship Between Social Activism and Feelings of Powerlessness Among Low Socioeconomic College Students. Journal of College Student Personnel, Vol. 15, No. 2, pp. 120-124, March, 1974.

Garrahan, D. Guidance Services Study. Leonia, NJ, 61 pages, July, 1973.

Morris, C. and Garrahan, D. Guidance Study Kit. Bureau of Guidance (N.Y.S. Education Department) and Institute of Field Studies (Teachers College, Columbia University), 1972.

Garrahan, D. An Analysis of the Relationship Between Feelings of Powerlessness and the Success of Socially Disadvantaged Students in Higher Education. Copyrighted Doctoral Dissertation, Teachers College, Columbia University, 1972.

Gordon, E., Garrahan, D., Bynum, E., and Lewis, A. Report on the Study of Collegiate Compensatory Programs for Disadvantaged Youth. Ford Foundation and the College Entrance Examination Board, 575 pages, 1972.

Garrahan, D. Friends of the East Harlem Block Schools. Concern, Vol. 10, No. 5, pp. 4-5, February, 1971.

Garrahan, D. In Support of Recruiting NEGROES. The Pocono Record (Stroudsburg, PA) Editorial Page, April, 1970.

Garrahan, D. Empathy and the Counseing Process: Historical Overview. Journal of the New York School Counselor Association, Vol. 2, No. 1, pp. 4-7, Spring, 1968.

Garrahan, D. How to Help the Forgotten Students in the School. N. J. Association of High School Councils, Yearbook, pp. 94-96, June, 1962.

PROFESSIONAL PRESENTATIONS

1995 National Conference of Christians and Jews (Youth Conference, Ramapo College of NJ, May 15, 1995) Plenary Session Moderator.

1991 National Conference of Christians and Jews (Spring Conference, Ramapo College of NJ, May 17, 1991) Program Coordinator and Workshop Leader (Control Orientation).

1986 N. J. Professional Counselors Association (Annual Spring Conference, Princeton, NJ, May 1, 1986) Invitational Address - "Pursuing Excellence: An Administrative Perspective."

8.

1983 Teaneck Board of Education (In-service Workshop - 15 sessions)
Workshop Leader: "Human Relations in Education - Teachers as Helpers," October 1983 - January 1984.

1981 Economic Development Council of N.Y.C. Participating Speaker Award, June 11, 1981.

1980 Eastern School for Physicians' Aides. Commencement Address, September 27, 1980.

1978 Institute of Gerontology (College of Misericordia, PA, Feb. 16-17, 1978)
Seminar Leader: "Psychological Intervention with the Aged."

1978 American Personnel and Guidance Association (National Convention: Washington, D.C., March 1978). Presenter: "Sex Equality in Educational and Vocational Guidance," Convention Program #494, p. 70; Abstracts p. 198.

1978 American Personnel and Guidance Association (National Convention: Washington, D. C., March, 1978) Presenter: "Designing Socially and Psychologically Supportive Environments for the Aged," Convention Program #166, p. 44; Abstracts p. 50.

1977 Denmark's International Educational Forum (Teachers College, Columbia University, June 29, 1977). Speech: "Counseling in American Schools."

1977 Title IX Conference (Lake George Central School District and BOCES Regional Planning Center, April 13, 1977). Title IX Consulting Speaker: "Equity in Educational Guidance and Career Development."

1977 Title IX Conference (New York State Central Western Region, Rochester, NY, March 9, 1977). Title IX Consulting Speaker: "Affirmative Action Compliance: Sex-Role Stereotyping in Schools."

1977 Institute of Gerontology (College of Misericordia, PA, Feb. 8-9, 1977) Workshop Leader: "Counseling the Aged" and "Designing Ecologically Supportive Environments for the Aged."

1975 Association of Counselor Education and Supervision (National Convention: New York, NY, March, 1975) National Program Chairman

9.

1975 Old Forge High School (PA). Commencement Address, June 16, 1975.

1974 Educational Testing Service (Urban Education Conference: Princeton, NJ, June, 1975) Speech: "Locus of Control - Guidelines for Future Research."

1973 Florida Personnel and Guidance Association (State Convention: Miami, FL, November, 1973) Invitational Address: "Evaluating Guidance Services: Consumer Perceptions - Needs Assessment Approach," Convention Program #062, p. 19.

1973 Glen Rock Educational Symposium (Glen Rock, NJ, January, 1973) Speaker: "Evaluation - Making Public Schools More Responsive to the Changing Needs of Youth."

1972 College Entrance Examination Board (Regional Conference: New York, NY, February, 1972) Presenter: "Report on the Status of Minority Programs in Higher Education."

1970 College Entrance Examination Board (National Emergency Conference: Yellow Springs, OH, September, 1970) Presenter: "Higher Education for Poor and Minority Youth - the State of Affairs."

1965 New York Congress of Parents and Teachers (State Convention: Ithaca, NY, April, 1965) Workshop Leader: "P.T.A. - An Action Image."

1962 World Order Day (Belvidere Methodist Church, NJ) "The Importance of World Law."

1961 New Jersey Association of High School Councils (State Convention: New Brunswick, NJ, November 15, 1961) Seminar Speaker: "How the Student Council Can Help the Forgotten Students in the School."

SPONSORED RESEARCH

As a member of the graduate faculty of Teachers College, Columbia University, between 1972 and 1978, I sponsored fourteen successful doctoral dissertations; co-sponsored an additional twenty doctoral dissertations; and served as an oral examiner for numerous dissertations prepared by doctoral candidates in school administration, curriculum and supervision, and psychology. Following are several of the doctoral dissertations which I sponsored to successful completion:

1978 An Exploratory Study of the Nature of the Academic High Risk Students' Perceived Frequency of Selected Study Skills.

1977 The Development of an Inventory of Career Concerns for Non-College Bound Students and an Analysis of These Concerns as Perceived by Students, School Career Counselors, and Business People in the Community.

1977 An Assessment of the Need for Pupil Personnel Services as Part of the Secondary School System of Liberia.

1977 An Examination of the Relationship Between Locus of Control, Socioeconomic Choice, Individual Performance and Group Effectiveness in Human Relations Training.

1977 Secondary School Education and Employment in Nigeria: Implications for Career Guidance.

1977 College Selection and Its Relationship to College Satisfaction.

1977 An Analysis of Occupational Preferences of Secondary School Students in Guyana with Particular Reference to the Manpower Needs of the Country.

1976 Originality Training: A Method for Locus of Control Change.

1975 Auxiliary Services for High School: A Model for Change.

1975 An Investigation of Play Group Counseling.

HONORS AND RECOGNITION (post 1985)

1994 Northern Highlands honored at the White House reception as a Drug-Free School.

1.

1991	Acknowledged as a contributor to The Report of the Quality Education Commission entitled, All our Children: A Vision for N.J. Schools in the 21st Century, 1991, p. 51 Appendix of Contributors.
1991	Distinguished Educator Award: State Education Department. June 28, 1991.
1991	N.J. Council of Education: Inducted March 8, 1991.
1986-91	Northern Highlands Regional High School District cited in over a dozen regional, State, and national publications.
1989	Northern Highlands' Child Development Program included in National Resource Guide to School-based Family Support and Education Programs by Harvard University.
1989-90	D. Garrahan included in Who's Who in American Education.
1989	Northern Highlands' School Security Program featured in Perspective - N.J.A.S.A.
1987-88	D. Garrahan included in Who's Who in Educational Administration.
1988	Northern Highlands' Nursery School-Child Development Program featured in School Leader - N.J.S.B.A.
1988	Northern Highlands ranked among the Ten Best Public High Schools in New Jersey Monthly.
1988	Northern Highlands honored at White House Reception as an Outstanding Secondary School.
1987	Northern Highlands recognized by the U.S. Department of Education as one of 123 exemplary public high schools in the United States.
1986	Northern Highlands' Basic Skills Program included in a Compendium of Model Programs by the N.J. Department of Education.

AN EXAMINATION OF THE RELATIONSHIP BETWEEN LOCUS
OF CONTROL, SOCIOMETRIC CHOICE, INDIVIDUAL
PERFORMANCE AND GROUP EFFECTIVENESS IN
HUMAN RELATIONS TRAINING

by

Calvin H. Sturgies

Dissertation Committee:

Professor David P. Garrahan, Sponsor
Professor Joseph C. Grannis

Approved by the Committee on the Degree of Doctor of Education

Date_____

Submitted in partial fulfillment of the
requirements for the Degree of Doctor of Education in
Teachers College, Columbia University

1977

Dear Dave —

Thank you again for sharing your time, energy and work with me. I am also indebted to you for the new set of survival skills you helped me to develop in pursuit of the Ph.D.)

Cal

For my own selfish reasons I'm sorry you left the N.Y. area. INSTITUTIONALLY, your absence has left a gigantic hole at Columbia & I suspect that Jordan will try to hire three people to "replace" you.

www.ingramcontent.com/pod-product-compliance
Lightning Source LLC
Chambersburg PA
CBHW080606170426
43209CB00007B/1343